Car Racing
Against
the Clock

CAR RACING AGAINST THE CLOCK

The Story of the World Land Speed Record

Frank Ross, Jr.

illustrated with photographs and drawings

Lothrop, Lee & Shepard Company / New York

A Division of William Morrow & Company, Inc.

*This book is dedicated with warmest affection
to my good friend, Master Dyke Joline*

1   2   3   4   5   80   79   78   77   76

Library of Congress Cataloging in Publication Data
Ross, Frank Xavier
  Car racing against the clock.

  Bibliography: p.
  Includes index.
  *SUMMARY: A history, emphasizing famous cars and drivers, of the continuing
attempts to drive the fastest car in the world from the 1898 record speed of
thirty-nine miles per hour to today's speeds of over 600 miles per hour.*
  *1. Automobiles, Racing—Speed records—Juvenile literature.
2. Automobile racing—Biography—Juvenile literature. [1. Automobiles, Racing—
Speed records. 2. Automobile racing—Biography] I. Title.*

GV1030.R67   796.7'2'0922 [B] [920]   75-38965
ISBN 0-688-41743-4   ISBN 0-688-51743-9 lib. bdg.

Contents

Introduction

The years immediately before and after 1900 were exciting ones in the field of technology. Rapid advances were taking place in methods of manufacturing, in communications, and in the production of power (electricity, for example). Some especially fascinating developments were occurring in the field of transportation, mainly because of the newly created automobile which promised to revolutionize the existing means of traveling.

Until the advent of the motor car in the late 1800s, the fastest way of traveling on land, excluding the railroad, was by horse and buggy. With the invention and development of the automobile, it became possible to travel on roads at more than double a horse's speed. This was particularly exciting to sports-minded people. They now had available a new, revolutionary machine that could test their technical knowledge and skills to a fascinating degree.

This testing took place in three important ways. Motor cars were raced against other motor cars on public roads; automobiles were raced on restricted tracks; and finally, automobiles were raced against the clock to find out how fast the horseless carriage could travel over a specified distance. It is interesting to note that all three of these different kinds of automobile tests came into existence at about the same time—late in the nineteenth century. And all three continue to excite both participants and spectators, more than three-quarters of a century later.

Over the years, automobile races that matched car against car underwent drastic changes. Autos changed radically in design, construction, and performance, and the rules by which auto races were run changed too.

The same evolutionary process took place in automobile races against time, in which drivers sought to establish world land speed records. That story is the subject of this book.

The quest for speed involves adventure, danger, skill, and daring. It is a story of steel-nerved men who did not rest until they had achieved their goal—to drive the world's fastest motor car.

The story also concerns the application of the most advanced technical knowledge to the design and building of super-swift automobiles. This began in the 1890s with the purring sound of electric automobiles rolling at the phenomenal speed of 65 miles per hour and continued to the present-day "big boomers"—turbo-jet and rocket-powered cars streaking at the mind-boggling rate of more than 620 miles per hour.

When will attempts to drive the world's fastest automobile end? No one can really say. As long as there breathes a person who strives to do the unusual, in spite of hazards, so long perhaps will the quest for the world's highest automobile speed continue.

Chapter 1
The First
Super-Speedsters

The automobile as a practical means of transportation was a little more than a dozen years old by the late 1890s. But there was already widespread interest in both Europe and the United States in the designing and building of automobiles. Enthusiasm also centered on racing motor cars in speed contests. Car racing in the early years reached its greatest popularity in France.

Autos of every description were designed and built by the French. The mechanical horseless carriage had caught their imagination and they became fascinated with the motor car's power and speed. There were French engineers and mechanics who felt that the superior automobile was propelled by an electric motor. Some held the view that a steam-powered car was best. Still other technicians were convinced that the motor car with a gasoline engine was far ahead of any other type. As a result of this variety of ideas, a great many different kinds of autos rolled along the city streets and country lanes of France.

But the competition among these various automotive ideas did not end with the building of different kinds of cars. Only by matching car against car in an actual speed contest could convincing answers be had. Thus two of the most exciting kinds of motor car competition came into existence.

The first of these matched automobiles against automobiles in road racing from one city to another. These races generated enormous interest among participants and spectators alike. The cross-country motor car races did a great deal to attract the public's attention to the horseless carriage's possibilities as a practical form of transportation.

The second kind of motor car competition involved racing automobiles against time over a certain distance. This type of motor car testing also originated in France and the established distance was set at one kilometer. How fast can an automobile travel over a specified distance? For more than three-quarters of a century daring drivers have been pushing themselves and their specially built machines to find the answer. In the course of this activity they have boosted the motor car's maximum speed to spectacular heights.

Racing an automobile against the clock over the distance of one kilometer began in December of 1898. Count Gaston de Chasseloup-Laubat, a wealthy French nobleman and a great sportsman, had a good deal to do with arranging this event. Only people of some financial means could afford to buy and maintain an automobile in the early days.

The count had been interested in motor cars from their very beginning. Soon after he acquired his first car, he eagerly sought to race it against those of his friends. His fascination with the motor car, and especially with racing, continued to grow; he joined with other motor car enthusiasts in 1895 to organize the Automobile Club of France, one of the first such groups in the world.

Chasseloup-Laubat favored the electric-powered motor car and was very proud of his Jeantaud, which had been designed and built by a small automobile manufacturer in Paris. The count liked the vehicle's silent operation and its lack of the smoke and obnoxious fumes produced by gasoline-driven motor cars. And the Jeantaud was extremely easy to operate. Simply by flicking a couple of switches, the driver could get under way. The Jeantaud was surprisingly fast for its day and had already brought the nobleman a number of victories in motor car races.

As autumn gave way swiftly to winter in 1898, the journal of the Automobile Club of France—*La France Automobile*—announced that the club would sponsor a new kind of automobile competition in which motor cars would be tested for top speed over a measured distance.

As soon as the article was published, applications to take part in the contest started to arrive in the club's office. Among the first was that of Count Gaston de Chasseloup-Laubat. Another came from Camille Jenatzy, a Belgian and one of the best-known racing drivers of that era.

The count and Jenatzy were no strangers to one another. They had competed in a number of automobile racing events. In some of these Jenatzy had driven gasoline-powered automobiles. However, for the particular competition announced in the journal, he planned to use an electrically propelled vehicle which he had designed. A big, jovial man with a fiery red beard, Jenatzy loved to joke with his rivals. When he learned that his old friend the count was entering the contest, Jenatzy told the nobleman to leave the Jeantaud at home—it had absolutely no chance of winning against his car.

The morning of December 18 had been chosen by the club for the running of the auto speed contest. The location was a little-used road—open, level, and hard-surfaced—in Achères Park, slightly north of Paris. Officials of the French auto club marked off two stretches of one kilometer each (1 kilometer equals 0.62 miles). The first was to be used by the contestants for a run from a standing start. Drivers were to place the front wheels of their vehicles on the starting line and then at the signal "go" take off for the finish mark.

The second of the kilometer stretches was to be used for a run from a flying start. Each car was to reach the starting line already traveling at full power and speed, and continue to the end. Timekeepers holding stopwatches were posted at the starting and finish lines of both kilometer stretches.

As matters turned out, Jenatzy did not appear for the competition. Business affairs needing his personal attention had called the racing driver back to Belgium. This, of course, put an end to the duel between him and the count. The latter came with his Jeantaud, which was now the only electric-powered car in the contest. All the others were propelled by gasoline engines.

The count's Jeantaud looked little different from the horse-drawn carriages of the day. Indeed, if a horse had been attached to its front end, the Jeantaud would not have attracted the slightest attention. It was box-shaped, square at the front and back, with two seats near the front end for the driver and a companion. The electric motor's energy came from a series of batteries that could not be recharged. Once their energy was gone, new batteries had to be installed in the automobile. They were enormously heavy, contributing over a third of the Jeantaud's total weight of 3200 pounds. The electric motor had a propulsion force equal to 36 horsepower.

A light rain fell on the day of the speed contest and a cold chill was in the air. Since the road surface was of compacted stones, its wetness was not expected to affect the speed of the cars. More than three hundred spectators had braved the unpleasant weather to watch the daredevils perform in their horseless carriages.

As the timekeepers signalled to the drivers, the gasoline-powered automobiles clattered and chugged one after the other over the kilometer distance. They were impressive for the noise they made and the reeking fumes of their exhausts. Their speed was an entirely different matter. Many were barely able to reach 30 miles per hour.

Chasseloup-Laubat then had his turn. The Jeantaud's electric motor permitted it to get away from a standing position at near top speed. Furthermore, the Jeantaud gave off no smoke and made very little noise. The only sound was the high-pitched hum of the electric motor. The count made his best run from the flying start. He covered the kilometer in 56 seconds for a speed of 39.24 miles per hour. None of the other competitors even came close to this mark, and the French nobleman was declared the winner. The count's speed mark was the first world record for an automobile over a measured distance.

The count's accomplishment caused little excitement among the general public. To automotive enthusiasts of the day, however, it

The electric-powered Jeantaud was the first automobile to estab-lish a world land speed record in 1898. The fashionably dressed Count Gaston de Chasseloup-Laubat is in the driver's seat.

PHOTO HUTIN-COMPIÈGNE

was exciting news indeed. Perhaps no one who heard of the event was more interested than Camille Jenatzy. He was confident that had he been at Achères, he would have driven off with the honors himself.

Jenatzy was so eager to prove that he had the fastest automobile in the world that he sat down immediately after reading about the count's triumph to write him a letter; it was a challenge to a match between the two sportsmen. The race would be run over the same course at Achères and under the same rules as the earlier competition. With complete confidence in his Jeantaud, Chasseloup-Laubat quickly accepted the challenge. The Automobile Club of France worked out the arrangements and provided a starting signalman and timers.

January 17, 1899, was the day chosen for the private auto duel. Jenatzy came to Achères with the electric auto he had designed and with which he had won a hill climbing competition the previous November. The count, of course, brought his record-holding Jeantaud. As the challenger, Jenatzy was given the courtesy of making the first runs. When he finished the standing start and the flying start, Jenatzy's best time was 41.42 miles per hour. He had broken the Frenchman's auto speed record just as he had boasted he would.

But the count was unruffled by Jenatzy's seeming triumph. He climbed into the driver's seat of the Jeantaud and prepared to roll to the starting line. He knew his car had power in reserve that would enable him to top the Belgian's mark. At the downward swish of the signalman's flag, the count snapped on the switch of his electric motor and almost immediately hit top speed, rolling silently and smoothly along the course. When the timers calculated their figures, the count had covered the distance at a speed of 43.69 miles per hour. The Frenchman was once again the auto speed king of the world.

After the count made his two runs, competition for the day came to an end. The Frenchman's auto had developed some mechanical trouble and could no longer run at full speed. Jenatzy was disappointed. He believed his car had extra power which would surely have made him the final victor. Now he had to wait for another opportunity to prove his car's superiority.

The thought bothered Jenatzy so much that in less than two weeks, on January 27, he returned to Achères Park alone. He was determined to capture the world auto speed crown even without the count's participation. With only officials of the auto club present, Jenatzy broke the old record by a wide margin—his speed was 49.92 miles per hour. This set off a seesaw battle between Jenatzy and the count for the world speed crown.

The French nobleman was quick to meet the new challenge. In February, driving the same Jeantaud, he tried to beat Jenatzy's new mark. A motor failure and a road surface roughened by frost, however, forced him to give up his speed record attempt.

Chasseloup-Laubat returned to Paris and took his Jeantaud to the factory where it had been built. He and the engineers and mechanics who had created the vehicle put their heads together to think of ways to increase its speed.

Someone pointed out that boats are designed with sharply pointed bows instead of blunt ones so that they can cut through the water more easily and speedily. Why not do the same with an automobile body? With a pointed nose, the auto would move against the air with less resistance. The idea met with instant approval and soon workers were busy with hammers and metal snippers forming a new streamlined body for the Jeantaud.

By the first of March the count's new electric auto was rolled out of the factory. It had not only a sharply pointed nose but a V-shaped tail as well. Three days later the French sportsman took it to the park at Achères in hopes of bringing the auto speed record back to France. His attempt was nothing short of sensational. He broke Jenatzy's mark by more than seven miles per hour, spinning smoothly and silently over the kilometer distance at a speed of 57.60 miles per hour.

Jenatzy had not been present at the shattering of his old record and he read about the count's achievement in the newspapers. He rose to the challenge immediately and began plans to regain the speed crown. Jenatzy noted how radically different the Jeantaud's new design was. Well, he thought, two could play at that game. The Belgian speedster had a few new ideas himself about the design of a record-breaking racing car. Soon he was working with his engineers and mechanics on a completely new road racer.

The auto was constructed under Jenatzy's watchful eye by a motor car manufacturer in Paris. When it was finished and rolled outdoors, the new racer's radical appearance caused quite a few raised eyebrows. It was a total break from the horse-and-carriage heritage.

The body of the car was cylindrical and pointed at both ends. It was made of partinium, a metal somewhat like aluminum that had recently been developed in France. The body was mounted on four small wheels with fat, air-inflated tires. Two powerful electric motors were attached to the rear axle, one alongside each rear wheel. They spun the wheels directly without the need of a sprocket chain, a feature of most early automobiles. The cargo of heavy batteries for powering the electric motors was placed inside the body. The electric motors were also of an improved type that could produce more power.

The driver's compartment near the rear of the vehicle was just big enough for a man to squeeze into. The car was steered by means of a long-handled tiller. One end of the tiller had an upright grip so the driver could apply more force when turning. Also within his reach were switches for starting the electric motors. The car had no brakes; it rolled to a stop after the electric power was consumed.

The position of the driver was rather awkward in that he sat

This is Camille Jenatzy in his electric-powered LA JAMAIS CON-
TENTE. PHOTO HUTIN-COMPIÈGNE

very high in the compartment. The lofty perch caused him to
receive the full blast of the wind during a high-speed run. But it
also gave him an excellent view of the road ahead. Jenatzy called
his little streamlined racing car *La Jamais Contente*—"the never
satisfied." This was Jenatzy's motto with respect to automobile
speed records.

Eager to show what his rolling bullet could do, Jenatzy brought
it to the park at Achères on April 1, 1899, where a new speed
course had been established. But his eagerness proved his undo-
ing. Before the timers could get into position, Jenatzy had turned
on the electrical switch and hummed over the measured kilometer.
Annoyed when told that the run had not been timed, Jenatzy had

Camille Jenatzy poses in his victorious LA JAMAIS CONTENTE *after setting a world speed record of 65.79 miles per hour in April, 1899.*　　MUSEO DELL'AUTOMOBILE TORINO

to call an end to the trials for the day. The electric batteries were exhausted and the car had to be returned to the factory for a new set.

Although the test run had not counted, Jenatzy was highly pleased with the way *La Jamais Contente* had performed. The Belgian felt certain that his speed had been far in excess of the count's mark. After some minor adjustments to his little racer and with new batteries installed, Jenatzy was ready for another try at the automobile speed record. He returned to Achères on April 29 and this time held his impatience in check until the officials of the Automobile Club of France could get into position.

Jenatzy made two test runs—from a standing start and from a flying start. The latter was his best try and the one that brought him the auto speed crown for the third time. His speed over the measured distance was clocked at 65.79 miles per hour. This was almost ten miles an hour faster than the mark set by the count. For automobile enthusiasts of the day, the Belgian's achievement was nothing short of sensational. As far as the Count de Chasseloup-Laubat was concerned, Jenatzy's new speed mark was too formidable to challenge. The French nobleman had to remain content with the part he had already played in raising the automobile's world speed record.

Chapter 2
New Racers
—New Records

During the automobile's early years, the electric motor was its most popular source of power. It was easily adapted for powering an automobile and so simple to operate that even people without the slightest knowledge of mechanics could quickly learn to drive electric cars.

The steam engine was almost as popular as the electric motor for propelling automobiles at the turn of the century. The principles on which the steam engine operated were well understood and there were a number of different kinds in use. Steam engines were employed for driving locomotives, powering factory machines, and producing electricity. Thus it was not too difficult for technicians in the early decades of this century to make another kind of steam engine for propelling an automobile.

The third of the main units for powering motor cars at the beginning of this century was the gasoline engine. Like the motor car itself, this was a relatively new invention. When it first came into existence, the gasoline-powered engine was noisy; it produced clouds of smoke and fumes and was extremely unreliable. The engine was difficult to start and once started, it was likely to stop frequently without warning. Its one big advantage was the greater power it could produce. This factor eventually made it the favorite power unit for cars used for racing.

But before gasoline engines completely took over the competition for world auto speed records, the steam power units were to have their day of glory. Their first victory came in 1902, just three years after Jenatzy had set his towering new auto speed mark with his electrically-powered car.

Léon Serpollet was a French inventor who was attracted to the possibilities of using the steam engine for motor car propulsion. He developed a compact steam boiler, capable of producing instant steam for power and small enough to fit the limited space of an automobile body. The flash boiler, as it was called, made super-heated steam by running water through a hot coiled metal tube.

This is one of the steam cars Léon Serpollet designed and built for the general public. PHOTO HUTIN-COMPIÈGNE

Serpollet connected his steam engine to a mechanical system for driving the rear wheels of his motor car. This resembled Jenatzy's *La Jamais Contente* in that it was pointed at both ends. But Serpollet's automobile was not cylindrical. Being flat on top and bottom, it was more boatlike; the Frenchman called it *La Baleine,* "the whale."

The body of Serpollet's steam car was mounted on a framework, or chassis, to which four rubber-tired wheels were attached. The driver's compartment was unusually large with the steering wheel and controls all located on the right-hand side. But Serpollet did not equip his steam car with brakes; it rolled to a stop after the driver shut off the steam engine. It seems that the French inventor built his steam car with just one goal in mind—to make it the fastest vehicle on wheels.

Serpollet was ready to test his steam auto at Nice, France, during the Easter holiday of 1902. One of the great attractions of that holiday period was a series of automobile races and speed contests that continued for almost a week. These included hill races in which drivers tried to get to the top in the fastest time and races of one car against another along flat stretches of roadway. Racing against time, for the fastest possible speed over a kilometer distance, was another top event and the one Serpollet planned to enter.

April 13 was the day of the kilometer speed competition. A kilometer distance was marked off on the Promenade des Anglais. Strollers were warned to stay clear of the course as the racing drivers prepared to mount their mechanical steeds. Serpollet with his "rolling tea kettle," as it was popularly called, was about to challenge some of the best-known racing cars of that era—Panhards, Mors, and Mercedes. All of these vehicles were powered with gasoline engines. But the French inventor was unworried.

After receiving the signal from the timers, Serpollet ignited his steam engine some distance back of the starting line. Several cars had preceded him but they had done poorly and Jenatzy's speed record still stood. Serpollet flicked the switches and, with puffs of white steam trailing behind, began to move. Rolling faster and faster, he flew across the starting line and headed for the finish marker under full steam. Unlike the rumbling roars from the gasoline-powered cars, only a faint hissing sound from the engine accompanied Serpollet's "tea kettle."

Serpollet's LA BALEINE.

Serpollet traveled swiftly along the Promenade straight as an arrow. He saw the signalman drop the flag at the finish line, but having no brakes, the Frenchman just kept on rolling at top speed. After shutting off the steam engine, he had to wait for his car to stop of its own accord. Fortunately, he had enough room to roll and nobody got in his path.

Finally, *La Baleine* came to a stop. Serpollet climbed quickly out of the driver's seat gasping for air. Fumes from his engine had blown back into the cockpit and made it difficult for him to breathe. The Frenchman made his way to the timers as quickly as he could and asked anxiously for the results. They gave him the happy news that he had just set a new world automobile speed record of 75.06 miles per hour! This was truly an astonishing mark, since only four years earlier the top speed for an automobile had been a mere 39 miles per hour.

Serpollet was enormously pleased. He had not only achieved the distinction of being the world's fastest driver of a motor car but he had accomplished this with an automobile of his own design and construction.

The speed record that Serpollet established did one thing in a very final way. It ended for all time the participation of electric-powered cars in such events. The speed needed to surpass 75 miles per hour was just too great for electric cars to attain. The only car with any chance of breaking the 1902 world land speed record was the gasoline-powered automobile. The gasoline engine was being rapidly improved in power and reliability and in the years immediately ahead would become a powerful challenger to the steam car.

If Léon Serpollet thought he would remain the world's automobile speed king for very long, he was in for a shock. His record was a challenge that other auto speedsters of the day lost little time in accepting, launching their efforts not with electrics or steamers but with gasoline-powered vehicles. Engineers were rapidly improving the cars themselves, as well as the gasoline engine, for greater power and reliability.

One of the most popular gasoline-powered racing automobiles of this period was the French-built Mors. This was a great brute of a machine whose thundering motor echoed along the country roads in many an intercity race.

A close second to the Mors, both in popularity with race drivers and as a winner of competitions, was another French-built auto, the Panhard. But the scourge of the road races during the early decades of this century was the Mercedes, designed and built by German engineers and mechanics. This roaring mechanical demon showed its tail to many competitors in races throughout Europe and America.

These three were among the best of the gasoline-powered motor cars, especially for racing. There were some others, of course, with names like Gobron-Brillié, Darracq, and Napier. It sometimes seemed that everyone with some mechanical talent and with an enthusiasm for speed and power felt he could build a motor car superior to any other. Many discovered this was not an easy task and quickly went out of business. Others took a little longer to fade away. A very few companies, like Mercedes in Europe and Ford in the United States, survive to this day, building automobiles to serve the transportation needs of the general public.

Road races and attempts at establishing new auto speed records were important in determining whether an automobile manufacturer continued in business. An automobile that consistently won races brought a manufacturer publicity, prestige, and all-important sales. On the other hand, if a motor car lost too frequently in competitions, the manufacturer might be forced to close the doors of his factory.

Besides serving as a showcase for a manufacturer's product, intercity auto races and efforts to establish new world speed records were significant for quite another reason. They led rapidly to one technical improvement after another in automobile performance. To outdo competitors, engineers often worked late over their drafting boards, thinking of new and better ways to get more power, speed, and reliability from the gasoline engine. New methods were devised for transmitting the engine's power to the car's driving wheels, eventually leading to the abandonment of chains for the drive shaft. Technical specialists employed by tire companies worked with equal vigor to make air-inflated tires more dependable. Tires were one of the major weaknesses of the early automobiles, whether for racing or normal transportation, and flat tires were an expected, common occurrence. As a result of all these intense technical efforts, the performance of automobiles, especially those powered by gasoline engines, improved almost daily.

While the horseless carriage captured a very large measure of attention in Europe, where it was invented, there was equally intense interest in it in other parts of the world. The United States, for one, had its fair share of auto enthusiasts, both in designing and building motor cars and in racing them. One of the earliest and best-known racing buffs was William K. Vanderbilt, a multi-millionaire sportsman.

Vanderbilt lived for long periods in France, and when automobile racing became the rage in Europe he was caught up in the excitement and danger of the sport. He got to know some of the most famous racing car drivers of the time and became familiar with the best automobiles for racing, keeping in close touch with the latest automotive technical developments. When Vanderbilt decided to join the fun of competing in the many auto races held in Europe, his great wealth enabled him to buy the most powerful and fastest motor car available.

It was not his money, however, that enabled Vanderbilt to win races against rough competition. The American sportsman soon proved his skill in driving high speed cars. When Vanderbilt returned to the United States, he brought his great enthusiasm for the European intercity road races with him, establishing the Vanderbilt Auto Cup Races that were first run on Long Island. These became enormously popular with spectators and participants alike. The races were international competitions in which the best drivers and cars of Europe and the United States thundered over the country roads.

Although Vanderbilt was a great enthusiast of road racing, he was also deeply interested in setting world auto speed records.

After reading about Serpollet's achievement, the American sportsman was sure that the powerful Mercedes he owned could do
better. The car was the very latest in a series of gasoline-powered
racers made by the German manufacturer. One day in April,
1902, shortly after Serpollet set his new world speed record,
Vanderbilt took his big motor car to a lonely country road in
France and proceeded to roar at top speed over the kilometer
distance. The best he could get his car to do, however, was a
disappointing 68 miles per hour.

But Vanderbilt was not one to give up easily. He felt confident
that his powerful machine had the speed to equal if not better
Serpollet's record. And so a few days after his first try, Vanderbilt drove his Mercedes to another lonely French road and again
opened the throttle wide. But the American sportsman was disappointed a second time. While he exceeded his first speed run,
Vanderbilt could only get up to 69 miles per hour. This was still
a long way from the 75 miles per hour record set by Serpollet.

Displeased but not discouraged, Vanderbilt now became completely absorbed in the challenge of breaking the auto speed mark.
He decided to make another attempt, this time using a French-built
Mors, the second of his favorite high-speed automobiles. Vanderbilt had driven this mechanical monster in the Paris-Vienna cross-
country race; while the car had not come in first, it had performed
to Vanderbilt's great satisfaction.

On August 5, 1902, Vanderbilt made arrangements with the
Automobile Club of France to have official timers check his speed
run on the Ablis-St. Arnoult country highway. The kilometer distance was marked off with flags and timers stationed at the
beginning and end. At the signal "go," Vanderbilt and his big
Mors rumbled to a start. He entered the kilometer stretch moving
at top speed and holding the steering wheel with all his strength.
There was no power steering in the automobile's early years and
a driver needed lots of muscle to hold his machine on the road.

Belching smoke and fumes, Vanderbilt's huge Mors roared over the required distance. He brought his juggernaut to a halt, then made his way to the stopwatch holders and anxiously asked for the results. This time the news was a joy to hear. Vanderbilt had covered the measured distance at a speed of 76.08 miles per hour.

Vanderbilt had not triumphed over Serpollet by a very wide margin. His victory was significant, however, in that a gasoline-powered vehicle had captured the world automobile speed record for the first time. The gasoline engine as a motive force for the horseless carriage had at last forged ahead of electric and steam power. As the gasoline engine was technically improved in the years ahead, it became the motor car's chief means of propulsion and has remained so right up to the present.

Vanderbilt enjoyed his world speed record for only a few months. In November of 1902 two French daredevils of the road —first Fournier, one of the great auto race drivers of the day, and then Augières—pushed the automobile speed record to 76.60 and then 77.13 miles per hour respectively. Both drivers used the same kind of motor car to achieve their records—a newly built, powerful Mors.

The rivalry to establish new auto speed records became so intense in this period that it attracted almost as much interest as the enormously popular intercity road races. Although French automobiles continued to dominate the speed record events, French drivers did not. The racers hailed from several different countries where the desire to wear the world auto speed crown was as strong as in France.

Following in the path blazed by Vanderbilt, the next non-Frenchman to establish a world auto speed record was a Belgian, Arthur Duray. In fact, he set two new marks, both in 1903. In his speed attempts, Duray sat behind the wheel of a Gobron-Brillié, designed and built in France.

This Mors model was driven to several world records, including the record speed of 77.13 miles per hour set by Augières in 1902.

This was a most unattractive looking machine even by the automotive standards of the early twentieth century. Appearance, however, was not important to Duray. The automobile had a newly designed gasoline engine that produced plenty of power and speed in the car's test drive. In July, 1903, Duray took his powerful vehicle to the beach at Ostend, Belgium. On the wet but firm sands Duray made his first effort at setting a new world auto speed record.

Approaching the start of the measured distance at flying speed, Duray opened the throttle to its widest position. Trailing sand, smoke, and a rumbling roar, the Belgian driver whipped over the course at a speed of 83.47 miles per hour. He had beaten the previous record by a margin of more than six miles per hour.

Duray was highly pleased with his accomplishment; looking over the racing car field at the time, he felt confident that no

The Gobron-Brillié was famous for its speed and its ability to consume huge quantities of gasoline. This model set two world speed records in 1903.

vehicle in sight could depose him as the world's speed king. However, he basked in this feeling of triumph for only a few weeks. Then he received a rude shock one day when he read about a speed attempt by an Englishman, Charles Rolls. Destined to make his name famous in the automotive world, Rolls had driven a Mors to a reported record speed of 84.73 miles per hour. But when officials of the French automotive club learned of the conditions under which he had made his run, they ruled that these were not in accordance with the club's standards and refused to recognize the Englishman's mark.

At about this same time another powerful Mors was driven to a near record speed mark of 84.09 miles per hour at Dublin, Ireland. But this attempt too failed to gain recognition by French auto club officials, for the speed run had not been made under club rules.

Whether these speed marks were official or not, Duray decided that competitors were getting much too close to his speed crown. He took his Gobron-Brillié to an official French automobile club kilometer course at Dourdan, France, and tried to improve his old speed record. The best Duray could do, however, was 84.73 miles per hour, only 4/10 of a second or .16 miles per hour faster than his run at Ostend; this was the same as Charles Rolls's reported speed.

Duray's speed attempt at Dourdan marked the end of such activity in 1903. In the following year, new cars and new drivers would enter the contest for the world auto speed record.

Chapter 3
American
Speedsters

In 1904 the scene of auto speed attempts shifted to a completely new location—the United States. Many Americans were as deeply interested in the automobile's development as their European counterparts. And they had just as much mechanical knowledge as those on the other side of the Atlantic Ocean. If there was a difference between automotive activity in Europe and America, it lay in the European fascination with racing. In America the emphasis seemed to be on the use of automobiles for transporting the public. Racing, especially intercity speed contests, never reached the same level of popularity in the United States as it did in Europe.

Of the many American pioneers in the development of the automobile, Henry Ford was undoubtedly one of the most outstanding. He was a mechanical wizard with a shrewd business sense. As a very young man Ford became involved with the development of the horseless carriage. He clearly saw the future possibilities of the automobile as a practical means of transportation. Fired by ambition, Ford dreamed of one day putting all America on wheels—and he almost did.

Henry Ford's mechanical and industrial genius brought the automobile within the financial means of many Americans, making it no longer merely a plaything of the wealthy. And the motor car with which he accomplished this was his famous Model T, affectionately known as the "Tin Lizzie." The Model T was a familiar sight on practically every highway and country lane in the United States right up until the 1930s. This historic Ford car is now a prized possession of many antique auto clubs and museums, and the automobile dynasty that Henry Ford founded continues to this day.

When Henry Ford first set up his automobile manufacturing business it was pretty much of a solo effort. In addition to making horseless carriages, he was also involved with their sale and promotion. Along with other American car manufacturers, Ford advertised his autos to the general public by displaying them at shows held in large cities throughout the United States. Ford, however, went a step further than most other car builders. He raced his cars in competitions. He had an exceptionally keen appreciation of the advertising value of such contests in arousing interest in motor cars and stimulating sales. Ford not only planned races and attempts to set speed records, but he actually took part in these himself. It was in this way that the American automobile pioneer became a participant in the international battle to drive an automobile faster than anybody else in the world.

Winter was hardly the time to find a road suitable for driving an automobile at high speed. Snow and icy ruts were normal conditions on Michigan roads in January. But Henry Ford was an extremely resourceful individual and determined to make automobile news. The idea came to him to use the frozen surface of a lake for his speed run. Solid and smooth, this frozen speed course seemed to present no problems. Ford had only to be sure that the lake's surface was strong enough to hold the weight of his racing vehicle; it also had to be long enough to permit a flying start and to provide sufficient room for stopping after crossing the finish line.

Ford investigated the many lakes around Detroit and finally decided on Lake St. Clair. For his attempt at a speed record Ford planned to use the Arrow, the second of his racing cars. His first racer, the 999, was more famous as the result of frequent wins on racing tracks. The Arrow was a kind of experimental car on which the automotive wizard tried out new mechanical ideas.

The Arrow had little resemblance to an automobile of today, or even to most of the motor vehicles of the early 1900s. It was simply a frame or chassis equipped with four wheels and a bulky

Henry Ford standing beside his most famous track racer, the 999. Barney Oldfield, a renowned racing driver of the early 1900s, is at the tiller. Steering wheels were not standard equipment on the early cars.

engine. Behind the engine, in about the middle of the chassis, was a simple bucket seat for the driver. In front of the driver were the steering wheel and controls for accelerating and stopping the vehicle. A crude metal windshield was fixed to a frame in front of the driver for protection against wind blast and engine exhaust. The car had no body covering over the engine or fender guards around the wheels.

The Arrow's construction was extremely simple, and yet it gave the appearance of fleetness. The car's wheels, large in diameter with wire spokes and thin tires, probably contributed a great deal to its look of swiftness.

Shortly after the first of January, 1904, Henry Ford and his mechanics rolled the Arrow from the factory and began tuning it up for the speed run. Its huge four-cylinder engine of 70 horse-power was tinkered with until the roar of its exhaust sounded pleasing to the mechanics' ears. Wheels and steering system were checked with extra care and by January 12 the Arrow was pronounced ready for its speed test. Ford had decided that he himself would hold the wheel of the Arrow during the run.

A mile distance was measured on the most acceptable part of Lake St. Clair. Since the icy surface presented a slipping problem for the Arrow's tires, especially for the start of the run, warm ashes were scattered about by Ford's assistants. After a last-minute adjustment to the engine by his top mechanic, Spider Huff, Ford was ready to go. He warmed up the engine for a few minutes some distance from the starting line, since he planned to enter the mile stretch at full speed. The roaring, rumbling sound of the massive engine echoed over the frozen lake.

Ford sat in the bucket seat with both hands gripping the steering wheel firmly. His peaked cap was pulled low over his eyes, which were protected with goggles. The collar of a warm coat had been yanked up to his ears on this cold, wintry day. At a signal from the starting timekeeper, Ford slipped the clutch of his

Henry Ford in the seat of the Arrow, waiting for his mechanic to make final adjustments before the start of his world record run on January 12, 1904.

COURTESY OF THE FORD ARCHIVES, DEARBORN, MICHIGAN

Arrow, put it in gear, and started to roll. Opening the throttle wider and wider, he moved with increasing speed over the ice.

By the time Ford reached the starting line, the Arrow's engine was rumbling at full power. Ford was hunched over the steering wheel, pushing the throttle to its limit. He zoomed into the opening stretch of the measured mile, surprising the tiny group of onlookers with his speed. The small windshield gave him little protection from the frigid wind. But even worse, and to Ford's great surprise, the ride was a very rough one. The icy surface was not as smooth as it appeared to the eye. There were tiny ridges, hard as granite, and cracks that the spinning wheels caught and magnified into a continuous succession of teeth-jarring bumps.

There were no seat belts in those days and as the Arrow bounced into the air and landed with a skidding jolt, Ford had all he could do to hang on. But he did it somehow and guided the Arrow at full tilt across the finish line. As the automobile genius proudly recalled later, "When I wasn't in the air I was skidding, but somehow I stayed topside up and on the course, making a record that went all over the world." *

Ford continued for some distance beyond the finish line before he was able to bring the Arrow to a halt. Then he turned around and headed back over the course to the timekeepers who were busily calculating the speed of his run. As he approached the timers and saw their smiling faces Ford knew before they spoke a word that his dash had been a record-breaker.

After climbing down from his seat on the Arrow, Ford walked to the timekeepers and asked for his time. To his great delight, he was told he had covered the mile in 39.4 seconds for a speed of 91.37 miles per hour—a new world record.

Henry Ford's speed record made automobile news throughout the United States, just as he had expected it would. And the publicity was exactly what Ford wanted: he planned to introduce his new car model to the public in February at a national auto show in New York City. However, when news of his record reached Europe and the ears of the officials of the French automobile club,

* From *Land Speed Record—A Complete History of World Record-Breaking Cars from 39.24 to 600+ MPH* by Cyril Posthumus (New York: Crown Publishers, Inc., 1972), page 28.

their reaction was wholly negative. Considered an official international group for conducting speed record attempts by automobile drivers, they refused to recognize Ford's achievement. He had not made his speed run according to the rules of the club and no official representative of the club had been present to observe the run.

Ford was not too disturbed by the ruling of the French auto club. His speed dash had been made in the presence of representatives of the American Automobile Association, an official automotive group in the United States that supervised auto races and kept records, and that was good enough for Henry.

The problem of international recognition of American speed records was to come up again and again in the years ahead. It caused a great deal of unpleasantness and confusion before the problem was finally cleared up by officials of both the French and American auto clubs. In the meantime, the failure to receive international recognition for their speed record attempts did not bother Henry Ford or any of the other American drivers who sought to crack Ford's mark. One of the first to make his effort was the perennial pursuer of automobile speed records, William K. Vanderbilt.

Vanderbilt, or "Willie K" as he was popularly known in the sporting world, had bought one of the latest of the Mercedes automobiles of 1904. The German-built vehicle was a superb engineering product with extremely pleasing lines. Gleaming white, the car had an engine of four massive cylinders churning out 90 horsepower. This impressive output was harnessed to the rear propelling wheels by sprocket chains, an arrangement similar to that of a bicycle. To break the force of the onrushing wind against the driver during a speed run, a special shielding was installed over the rear portion of the motor hood. Actually, this was an attempt at streamlining, which was increasingly recognized by automotive engineers as an important factor in reaching top speeds.

Barely two weeks after Henry Ford set his auto speed record, Vanderbilt was ready to try to break it. However, he had no desire to make his test run in the frigid north. Instead, Willie K took his big, powerful Mercedes to Florida and looked for a place to make his speed run. He found what he wanted at Daytona Beach, where other drivers had been racing their roaring juggernauts for several years.

Daytona Beach, with its wet but firm sandy surface, was a splendid place for driving motor cars at top speed. It was almost twenty miles long and wholly without obstructions. Daytona Beach subsequently became and remained for a number of years the world's best known course for automobile speed record efforts.

William K. Vanderbilt, Jr., drove a Mercedes like this one to a world speed record in 1904.

On January 27, 1904, Vanderbilt took his gleaming white Mercedes to a marked-out course on Daytona Beach and tried to topple Ford's speed record. The best he could do, however, after forcing the last ounce of power from his big machine, was 92.30 miles per hour. This was a new record but hardly one to delight

Willie K. He had topped Ford's mark by the slim margin of only one mile per hour.

Following Vanderbilt's capture of the automobile speed crown, the chase for new world speed records returned again to Europe. The great ambition of auto speed drivers now was to break through the 100 miles per hour barrier. This was finally achieved on July 21, 1904, on the sandy beach at Ostend, Belgium. The daredevil who accomplished this spectacular feat was the well-known French driver Louis Rigolly. To achieve his history-making run, Rigolly held the wheel of a Gobron-Brillié. The great brute of a machine carried the driver over the sands at a sizzling 103.55 miles per hour.

One might suppose that after the development of an automobile capable of speeding faster than 100 miles per hour, interest in continuing such technical activity would slacken. But such was not the case. If anything, that achievement seemed to stimulate those in love with fast automobiles to even greater efforts to increase their speed. The competition among auto builders and racing drivers continued at the same intense pace as before. And the speed challenges continued to seesaw back and forth across the Atlantic Ocean between European and American drivers.

One of this series of new speed records, set in 1906 by the American driver Fred Marriott, is interesting in terms of the motor car's history. Marriott's achievement was notable because his vehicle was steam-powered, at a time when automobiles with gasoline engines held a monopoly on the record speed runs. Léon Serpollet in 1902 had been the last to use a steam-powered car for a record run. After he lost the speed crown to a gasoline-powered automobile, it was thought that steam-powered cars would never compete in auto speed races again. The gasoline engine had progressed enormously in reliability and power so that in the period just before World War I, most autos on the public highways were propelled by gasoline engines.

However, there were two American motor car builders who did not accept the idea of the gasoline engine's superiority over the steam power unit. They were identical twin brothers, Francis and Freeland Stanley of Newton, Massachusetts. The Stanley brothers had developed and perfected a very good steam engine, small and powerful, for propelling an automobile. Stanley Steamers, as the cars became popularly known, were among the fastest on the road, and their speed made them extremely popular with the public. The Stanley factory at Newton was a busy place as the brothers tried to keep up with orders for their excellent steam cars.

Even though their business was good, the Stanley brothers did

The Stanley twins in one of their late nineteenth-century steam cars. AUTOMOBILE MANUFACTURERS ASSOCIATION

not relax in their efforts to improve it. Like Henry Ford, they knew that a little advertising could go a long way toward increasing sales. So the Stanley brothers decided to enter the international competition to build the fastest automobile in the world. They were confident that they could build a steam-powered auto that would outspeed the best of the gasoline-powered cars.

When the Stanley racer was finally unveiled, its appearance was strikingly like that of a canoe turned upside down and fitted with wheels. The boatlike body of the car was sharply pointed at both ends. It was constructed of wood and canvas and painted bright red. The car's similarity to a boat may have been the result of its body being constructed by boat builders; the knifelike front end of the car could cut through the wind just as a boat cuts through the water. The streamlined body was attached to extremely thin, wire-spoked wheels without fender guards.

The steam engine with which the Stanley brothers equipped their racer weighed almost 200 pounds. It was installed in the rear of the body close to the back wheels. The steam boiler, the engine's power source, was placed directly in front of the engine and was built to take 1000 pounds per square inch of pressure. The driver sat very low in the cockpit, almost on the floor of the vehicle in front of the steam boiler. His head barely came even with the edge of the front hood. Thus, he offered as little resistance to the wind as possible while traveling at high speed. The racer was guided with two vertical bars pushed back and forth, instead of a conventional steering wheel.

The vehicle was extremely light, scarcely more than 1600 pounds, which contributed to its racing capabilities. The Stanley brothers called their racer the Rocket, a name that reflected its phenomenal speed.

By January of 1906 the Stanley twins were ready to see what the Rocket could do. They shipped the auto to Daytona Beach, Florida, in time to take part in the automobile racing events that were held there annually. Called Speed Week, the various contests drew competitors from the United States and Europe. The biggest event of the week was an attempt by the driver of the most powerful automobile present to establish a new world speed record.

Fred Marriott, a member of the Stanley brothers' factory staff, had been chosen to drive the Rocket in the attempted record speed run. He was not a professional racing car driver but was familiar with handling high speed automobiles. In the course of the week's contests, Marriott acquired an excellent idea of what the Stanley Rocket could do. He had cracked no less than five records for various short and medium distance speed runs when he prepared to challenge the world automobile speed record. This event, the climax of Speed Week, was scheduled for January 23.

The mile and kilometer distances were measured off on the sands of Daytona Beach; timers took their positions and Marriott, some five miles from the starting line, sat quietly in the cockpit of his red racer waiting for the boiler of his engine to build up full steam pressure. The five-mile head start was needed for the Rocket to reach full power and speed by the time it crossed the starting line.

When the Rocket was at peak power, Marriott removed his foot from the brake pedal. The Rocket shot forward, trailing billowing clouds of steam. The slim car skimmed over the beach like a red streak. Marriott crossed the starting line at top speed, then continued to travel as swift and straight as an arrow in flight.

As he flashed over the finish line, an official pressed the button of his stopwatch at 28.2 seconds; Marriott had covered the mile stretch at the sensational speed of 127.66 miles per hour! This was a new world automobile speed record—but only for the Americans. French auto club officials again refused to accept the new mark, feeling that Marriott had not made his speed run under the proper rules of the club.

Despite the fact that the Rocket's achievement failed to gain international recognition, the Stanley brothers were so pleased with their car's performance that they eagerly began work on a new steam engine for the racer. More powerful than the Rocket's original engine—its boiler was designed to take 1300 pounds of pressure to the square inch as compared to 1000 in the earlier model—the new unit was expected to give the racing car far greater speed. The Stanley twins looked forward to the 1907 auto speed events at Daytona Beach and a still more sensational performance by the Rocket.

Fred Marriott again was given the job of guiding the steam Rocket. He was just as anxious as the car's builders to see what

This is the steam-powered Rocket designed and built by the Stanley twins. With Marriott behind the wheel, the car broke the world land speed record at Daytona Beach in 1906.

AUTOMOBILE MANUFACTURERS ASSOCIATION

it could do with the more powerful steam engine. A far larger audience than the previous year's gathering had come to the beach to watch the famous car perform.

The red Rocket's new steam engine needed a longer period to reach a full head of pressure—and thus top speed—so this time Marriott began his run seven miles from the starting line. Onlookers let out shouts of astonishment as he flashed down the beach and over the starting mark, a blurred red streak. As he later described his sensational ride, Marriott said, "I hit the measured mile wide open, and I glanced at the speedometer. It read 197 and was rising rapidly . . . Suddenly I hit something that felt like running into a curbstone . . . The car went up like a kite . . . She rose about 10 feet off the beach and traveled 100 feet before she struck . . ." *

Spectators were horrified to see the Rocket sail through the air, then crunch into the sand with a sickening thud and break in two. Apparently the mile stretch had not been examined carefully enough. Marriott, traveling at terrific speed, had been unable to swerve in time to avoid a rough spot in the sand and had lost control of his vehicle.

Rescuers dashed to Marriott's aid, dragged him unconscious from the wreckage, and laid him on the beach as gently as possible. Badly battered about the face and body, Marriott miraculously survived the accident.

The demolished Rocket put an end to the Stanley brothers' involvement with high speed racing cars. Thereafter they kept strictly to the business of making automobiles for the general public. Eventually, however, they went out of business because the gasoline-powered motor car proved too much of a competitor.

* From *The Fastest Men in the World—On Wheels* by Deke Houlgate and Editors of *Auto Racing Magazine* (New York: World Publishing Company/Times Mirror, 1971), page 14.

By the time World War I broke out, the world speed record for motor cars had been increased to 141.37 miles per hour. This last mark had been set by a rough and daring American dirt track driver, Bill Burman. For his record run on April 23, 1911, he drove a powerful Mercedes-Benz on the sands of Daytona Beach.

But Burman's record was not recognized internationally; once more the Automobile Club of France refused to accept the speed record as official because the American driver had not made the run in accordance with the new rules of the club.

One of the more drastic of these new rules dealt with the two-way running of a speed effort. Previously it had been sufficient for drivers seeking to establish speed marks to dash only once over a measured distance. Then officials of the French auto club had realized that some shrewd drivers were using tail winds to boost their speed. Depending on the wind's force, drivers could sometimes add a mile or more to a speed record.

The officials also became aware that speed courses were not always perfectly level. Some sloped in the direction of the finish line. This too could add speed to a driver's record attempt. If either a favorable tail wind or a sloping course were taken advantage of, an automobile's true top speed could not be determined.

Accordingly, French auto club officials decided that drivers attempting to break the world auto speed record would have to make two runs over the same course, one in one direction and the second in the opposite direction. The speeds made during the two runs would then be averaged and the resulting figure would be the one that really counted.

At first, this rule met with a good deal of opposition in both Europe and America. But in time it was recognized as reasonable and fair, and speed record attempts thereafter were made in accordance with the rule.

Attempts to raise the world speed record for automobiles came to an end with the outbreak of World War I in 1914. Auto racing of any kind did not resume until after the end of that conflict. When it did, a spectacular new chapter in the history of automobile land speed records was opened. Incredible machines were created to be driven by equally incredible, steel-nerved men.

Chapter 4
The British
Super-Speedsters

The Armistice on November 11, 1918, signalled the end of World War I. Three months later, in February of 1919, racing car drivers were back at their old game of pushing the automobile speed record to new heights. Ralph de Palma, an American star of road and track motor car racing, was the first of the postwar speed kings. Handling the wheel of a highly streamlined, powerful Packard racer, de Palma scorched the sands of Daytona Beach at a sizzling 149.875 miles per hour. He had beaten the old prewar world mark by more than eight miles per hour.

Part of the significance of de Palma's speed run lay in the mechanical features of the motor car he drove. The powerful twelve-cylinder engine, for example, had been designed for airplanes, not automobiles.

Ralph de Palma's Packard racer was the first of the record-seeking motor cars to reflect technological advances brought about by wartime demands. And yet, important as these were in helping to bring the speed crown to the American race driver, they were strictly elementary in the light of what was to happen during the 1920s. By that time World War I technology, with respect to motor power particularly, had been carried to new heights. When the extraordinarily powerful new engines were mated to motor cars designed to be the fastest in the world, they produced a remarkable family of machines. This new breed of high-speed motor vehicles ushered in the modern era of racing cars for land speed records.

Prior to World War I and for a short period thereafter, most of the auto speed records were achieved by French and American auto builders and drivers. But with the creation of modern, super-fast automobiles, this activity shifted to Great Britain. The British in the postwar decades became fascinated with the challenge of building and driving the world's fastest motor car. Indeed, this British absorption with speed was not limited to automobiles. Throughout the 1920s and 1930s they were just as deeply interested in piloting the world's fastest speedboat and flying the world's fastest airplane. At one time the speed crowns for all three categories—land, sea, and air—were held by the British. And the men who engaged in these highly dangerous activities were just as extraordinary as the vehicles they handled. They displayed iron will and a complete lack of fear in an extremely dangerous business. A number of them lost their lives in the quest for these speed crowns.

Major Henry O. Segrave and Captain Malcolm Campbell were among the best known of the British auto speedsters of the 1920s and 1930s. These two nerveless, daring sportsmen made the years 1927 and 1928 particularly exciting ones with their record-shattering, thunderous drives on Daytona Beach.

Henry Segrave was a retired British Army officer. Even before he chose to confine himself to the task of becoming the fastest man in the world with a motor car, Segrave had acquired a wide reputation as a superb and winning driver of racing cars in track competitions.

The machine with which Segrave hoped to set a new record was indeed a sensational looking member of the new breed of racing cars. Long and low, the vehicle weighed slightly more than four tons. Much of this weight consisted of two twelve-cylinder airplane engines. When the racer's throttle was fully opened, these huge propulsion units produced a combined output of 1000 horsepower.

The car's designers borrowed more than engines from the aeronautical field. They gave the massive machine a highly streamlined body for minimum wind resistance. The body was a metal shell that encased the entire vehicle including the wheels. It was rounded in front and tapered slightly at the rear.

Despite its very advanced mechanical features, Segrave's superspeedster had one connection with earlier racing cars. This was the chain linkage that transmitted the engines' power to the rear wheels.

Segrave's machine, painted bright red, was named the Sunbeam. Before it left the factory, it was subjected to an exhaustive test run. The racing car was put on a stationary power test rig and for many hours its engines were run at low and full throttle. At the end of the test, Segrave and his colleagues were convinced that they had built a winning automobile.

As he watched the huge automobile roaring full blast on the test stand, Segrave thought that the speed of the spinning wheels made them look like semi-invisible discs. With the help of a battery of instruments, the builders of the Sunbeam calculated the potential speed of the racer at more than 200 miles per hour.

Confident of the Sunbeam's power and fleetness, Major Segrave set two goals for himself in the upcoming test drive. The first, of course, was to break the existing world automobile speed record; the second was to become the first person ever to drive a motor vehicle faster than 200 miles per hour. Traveling at this sizzling speed required a course of enormous length; the only one in Great Britain was the beach at Pendine in southern Wales. Its nearly eight miles of wet firm sands had been used by other British drivers in search of a land speed record, including Captain Malcolm Campbell, Segrave's chief rival. Indeed, it was Campbell's record that Segrave hoped to break. Campbell had captured the speed crown on February 4, 1927, by roaring over the beach at Pendine in his swift Bluebird at a speed of 174.88 miles per hour.

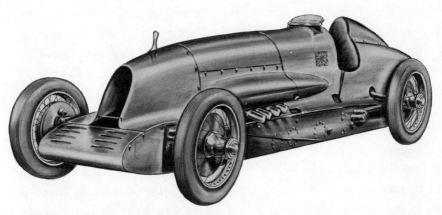

In 1927 Captain Malcolm Campbell set a new world land speed record of 174.88 miles per hour in his Napier-powered Bluebird.
THE BRITISH PETROLEUM CO., LTD.

However, after thoroughly discussing the question of where to hold the speed run, Major Segrave decided against Pendine. It was a disappointment to him as well as to his associates. They had hoped that a new speed record could be established on British soil. But the stretch of beach at Pendine was just not long enough for an automobile with the speed of the Sunbeam. Segrave had to be practical—his life was at stake even under the best of driving conditions. And so the decision was made to take the Sunbeam to Daytona Beach, Florida. By the late 1920s this long, firm stretch of beach had acquired international fame as an arena for speed record attempts. Only here, Segrave felt, could the enormous power and speed of his Sunbeam be unleashed to its fullest with a measure of safety.

Major Segrave knew that to break the existing world auto speed mark would not be easy. When Campbell and his Bluebird raised the figure to almost 175 miles per hour, many race car drivers felt that the upper limit of automobile speed had nearly been reached.

But there were others with quite an opposite view who believed that the automobile's speed limitations were nowhere near being approached and that the 200 miles per hour barrier would soon be crossed. Major Segrave was one of the strong supporters of this view.

After a restful crossing of the Atlantic Ocean and an overland railroad journey, Segrave and his small but enthusiastic crew of helpers arrived at Daytona Beach early in March, 1927. The Sunbeam was carefully uncrated. Several weeks were spent checking every bolt and piece of equipment. The utmost care was taken to prevent any failures in the course of the speed run. Even a minor mechanical failure could cause the streaking Sunbeam to roar out of control with grave danger to its driver.

When the engines of the super-racer were tuned to a smooth, rhythmic, rumbling sound, several practice runs were made over the beach. Finally, the Sunbeam was pronounced in top-notch condition. The time for performing had come. The day was March 29, clear and sunny. The course on the sandy beach had been inspected very carefully to make sure there were no bumps or ridges, and it had been marked with a double row of wooden poles. The runways had been measured for the flying mile, the kilometer, and the five-kilometer distances. With one attempt the Englishman hoped to set records in all three categories.

Thousands of spectators, having read of Segrave's intended assault on the world automobile speed record, lined the course. Guards along the route made certain that none strayed too close to the speeding automobile. The international rule was now in effect, and universally accepted, that a driver seeking the world speed crown had to make a run first in one direction and then in the opposite direction over the same course. Part of Segrave's crew of mechanics waited at the end of the course to give any help he might need for the return trip to the original starting line.

As Major Segrave climbed into the cockpit of the Sunbeam, his wristwatch showed it was nearly ten o'clock. The huge machine was towed far down the beach; Segrave would come up to the starting markers at almost full throttle. At a point several miles away from the starting flags, the powerful engines of the Sunbeam were started. They sputtered momentarily, then caught and burst into a deep, rumbling roar. Their thunderous sound carried easily to the distant spectators.

Satisfied with what he heard, Segrave released the brakes, shifted into gear, and began to roll over the firm sand. He picked up speed quickly and in seconds was flying over the beach. He shot across the starting line at a blistering speed, then straight as a bullet roared toward the finish line.

This is the snub-nosed Sunbeam in which Henry Segrave attempted to set a new world land speed record in 1927. He hoped to travel faster than 200 miles per hour.

THE BRITISH PETROLEUM CO., LTD.

Suddenly a blast of wind struck Segrave and his flashing red vehicle broadside. The car headed off course, out of control. Working the wheel furiously, Segrave tried desperately to bring his mechanical steed back onto the course. He finally got it under control and continued full tilt through all three of the measured distances. But his dangerous ride was not over yet.

As Segrave tore over the last of the finish lines, the Sunbeam again swerved out of control. For a second time the Englishman struggled with the wheel to regain command. Before he succeeded, the Sunbeam had snapped off several of the marker poles as though they were toothpicks. Then as Segrave slowed the giant motor car, he discovered that the brakes were not working properly; they were not stopping the fast-moving car quickly enough. Coolly, he headed the Sunbeam into the nearby surf. He hit the water with tremendous force, sending up a spectacular curtain of spray as the Sunbeam came to a halt.

Racing to his aid, crewmen found Segrave shaken but uninjured and undiscouraged by his close brush with death. He refused to give up driving for the day, as he was urged to. Instead, Segrave ordered a quick inspection of his racer for the return run. Hauling the huge machine back onto the beach, the mechanics put four new tires on the wheels and made the Sunbeam ready for the second dash.

Again starting a long way from the beginning marker, Segrave passed over it at almost full throttle. Spectators could see little more than a streak of red. At one point all heads were turned toward the starting line as the cry arose, "Here he comes!" In almost the same instant all heads swiveled in the opposite direction to the cry, "There he goes!"

Major Segrave took a quick look at his speed indicator. The pointer had passed the 200 mark! He was traveling faster than anyone had ever gone in an automobile. The only machines faster than Segrave's at that moment were airplanes, and even among

*Henry Segrave behind the wheel of his Sunbeam on the sands of
Daytona Beach.*

CHRYSLER UNITED KINGDOM, LTD./ROOTES MOTORS, LTD.

these skyborne vehicles there were not many that could reach this
velocity.

This time as he zoomed over the finish line, Segrave did not
experience the sickening feeling of riding in an uncontrollable
racing car. He was able to bring his machine to a halt within a
reasonable distance. Then he swung his Sunbeam around and
headed sedately for the little group of official timers. The English
sportsman was confident that he had smashed Campbell's record.
But what he wanted to hear most was the news that he had roared
through the 200 miles per hour barrier.

The timekeepers from the American Automobile Association,
the American counterpart of the French automobile club, were
still busily at work over the figures they had recorded. Segrave
sat quietly in his thunderbolt waiting to hear the results. His crew
of mechanics fussed over the Sunbeam, not because the car needed
attention but just to be doing something to ease the tension of

waiting. Then the officials shouted the good news to Major Segrave. He had set new records for all three speed categories. But the one he was most interested in was the flying mile; he had roared over this distance at the astonishing rate of 203.792 miles per hour!

News of Segrave's achievement spread quickly throughout the United States and Europe. Overnight, the daring Englishman became an international hero, particularly in the world of motor cars. Among the hundreds of messages of congratulation that he received, Segrave enjoyed one, perhaps, the most: Captain Malcolm Campbell sent warm praise for an excellent performance. But while Segrave basked in his hard-won glory, Campbell went quickly and quietly to work to regain his speed crown.

Malcolm Campbell was a man born to be perpetually in a hurry. While still in his teens he once displayed his love for speed by zipping down a hill on his bicycle at better than twenty miles per hour. There was nothing unusual about the performance except that Campbell flashed along with his hands high above his head instead of on the handlebars. The local police were not impressed with young Malcolm's speed stunt and gave him a summons.

During the years before World War I, the airplane was a new and sensational means of transport. Fragile flying machines and their daring pilots were making headlines in the newspapers almost daily. The excitement of this aerial activity caught Malcolm Campbell's imagination and he soon became deeply involved. He was still in his early twenties when he decided to build his own flying machine as well as fly it. However, his association with aircraft proved anything but a happy one.

The experience turned out to be enormously costly and extremely dangerous. Campbell crashed his flying machine so many times that he finally abandoned it. Although he managed to walk away from each crack-up with only minor injuries, he felt he was pushing his luck too far. He decided to concentrate on earth-bound vehicles—like the automobile.

Malcolm Campbell's close connection with racing cars began at the popular Brooklands track. This was one of the earliest of the closed circuits for motor car competitions in England. Campbell's skill and daring as a driver soon brought him winning honors.

When World War I began in 1914, Malcolm Campbell lost little time enlisting in the British forces. He became a dispatch rider, driving fast motorcycles and motor cars between the front lines and headquarters. Later, near the end of the war, Campbell switched to the flying service. By the time the conflict was over, he had risen to the rank of captain.

With the return of peace, Campbell engaged once more in track races, outwitting and outspeeding his competitors. However, he soon lost interest in this kind of racing and turned his attention to speed racing of quite a different type—attempting to drive the fastest motor car in the world. He focused all his energies on becoming the world's automobile speed king, and by 1927 he had held the honor three times. After being dethroned by Major Segrave, Campbell became a restless dynamo of action to re-capture his laurels.

In planning his attack on Segrave's newly established record, Campbell decided against building a completely new automobile. For one thing, building these highly complex speed vehicles had become extremely expensive. For another, he felt that the Blue-bird with which he had established the mark Major Segrave had topped was basically a sound automobile. Given a more powerful engine and additional streamlining of the body, Campbell felt confident that the Bluebird could do the job.

With equipment and ideas borrowed from the aviation field, the Bluebird looked quite different when it was rebuilt. An aircraft engine with almost twice the power of the older unit was installed, and the body was drastically changed with a sharply streamlined, tapered nose. The new design was expected to reduce the force of the air against which the car would push as it traveled at high speed. The most radical change, however, was the addition of a large vertical fin to the tail end of the car.

It had been noticed that as car speeds became faster and faster, the rear portion of a vehicle tended to swish from side to side. This action, while the racer was moving at top speed, was disturbing to the driver to say the least. It could lead to loss of control of the car and possible disaster. Captain Campbell and the engineers who worked with him felt that the airplanelike tail fin would stabilize the Bluebird even at very high speeds.

One other mechanical feature of Campbell's Bluebird set it apart from most other racing cars of the time. This was the mechanism used for transmitting the power from the engine to the driving wheels at the rear. A steel drive shaft replaced the sprocket chain device, which was now considered inefficient for the super-high speeds being achieved with motor cars.

In keeping with its name, the rebuilt Bluebird was painted a bright blue. Captain Campbell had a special fondness for this color and had used it on all his previous record-breaking cars.

After months of painstaking work, Campbell's rebuilt Bluebird was ready for the big test. Like his victorious competitor Major Segrave, Campbell felt that the best place for driving a mechanical thunderbolt capable of a top speed of more than 200 miles per hour was the unobstructed course at Daytona Beach, Florida. And so, arriving in America in the winter, Campbell was at Daytona in early February, 1928, overseeing the final adjustments to the Bluebird and the arrangements for the course and timekeepers. As with Major Segrave's run, the American Automobile Association took responsibility for timing the record speed attempt.

When Campbell arrived at Daytona, he was surprised to learn that he was not to be the only performer in quest of an automobile speed record. Two American racing car drivers, Frank Lockhart and Ray Keech, were also on the scene with super-fast automobiles, ready to challenge both Segrave's record and Campbell's, if the latter achieved a new mark.

The twenty-fifth anniversary of Speed Week was in progress when Campbell arrived in Daytona. The organizers of this motor car jamboree were delighted that the special occasion would be highlighted by the attempts of these three famous cars and drivers to capture the world automobile speed record.

Captain Campbell decided he was not going to be distracted from the job he had come to do by any carnival activity. If anything, the boisterous atmosphere at Daytona made him more restless than usual. He was anxious to get behind the wheel of his powerful Bluebird.

The winter weather had not been good for the sandy course at Daytona Beach. Strong winds almost daily and a wild ocean surf had made the beach rough and bumpy. The weather continued bad through much of February, with the winds blowing strong and steady. These could be dangerous to a speeding racer if they struck the vehicle at an angle, making it very hard to control.

As day after day passed with no letup of the steadily blowing wind, Campbell's patience ran out. Finally he decided to wait no longer and had the Bluebird rolled to the beach. Even if conditions were not good for a record speed try, at least he could give his blue thunderbolt a trial spin and a last-minute check.

Campbell warmed the Bluebird's engine for a few moments, then opened the throttle full. The thunderous roar echoed over the beach, delighting the spectators who had come to witness the test run. Even though Campbell was not trying for the record, it was thrilling to see the big, powerful Bluebird gliding swiftly over the sands.

Approaching the starting markers of the measured course, the Bluebird moved with the speed of a bullet. Its engine thrummed with a silky, smooth roar as Campbell opened the throttle for maximum power. As the needle on the speedometer moved closer and closer to the 200 mark, Campbell suddenly decided to go for the record. But as he flew over the sandy course, Campbell's Bluebird suddenly struck a rough spot on the beach. The racing car shot up into the air, then hit the beach with a sickening thud. Fortunately, it landed right side up. But the impact gave Campbell an awful jolt, almost catapulting him out of the cockpit. Using all his driving skill, the Englishman coolly brought his mechanical steed to a skidding halt. Not only was Campbell badly shaken but the Bluebird had suffered serious damage.

Bitterly disappointed by the mishap, Campbell and his crew worked long hours to get the Bluebird back to the beach as soon as possible. They wanted to try another speed run before the American drivers made their attempts.

By February 19 the Bluebird was again in top running condition. Despite a steady and strong wind, Captain Campbell, impatient as ever, took his Bluebird to the beach. He revved up the engine to a full thunderous roar. Satisfied with the sound, Campbell released the brakes and headed for the starting line of the measured course several miles away.

The English sportsman zoomed up to the starting flags like a shot out of a cannon. He pressed down still harder on the accelerator and the Bluebird leaped ahead even faster. Campbell took a quick look at his speedometer and saw the needle pass the 200-mile mark. When he had climbed into the Bluebird, Captain Campbell had planned only to give the repaired racer a trial run. But now, streaking beautifully at more than 200 miles per hour, he again decided to make the run an official try for the record.

The more gas Campbell fed his engine, the more swiftly the Bluebird skimmed over the beach. The needle on the speedometer hit the 210 mark, passed it, and climbed steadily until it pointed to 215 miles per hour! By this time Campbell had roared over the finish line and was beginning to bring his blue thunderbolt to a halt. Once again, however, without warning the vehicle struck a shallow gully in the beach. All four wheels of the racer left the ground.

Campbell was nearly flung from his seat by the shock. He grabbed the steering wheel with all his strength. Then, as the Bluebird crashed back to the beach, he worked the brake pedal to bring the monster machine under control. It finally came to a skidding halt, plowing long, deep furrows in the sand with its rear wheels.

The impact left Campbell momentarily stunned. He found too that his back and one arm had been badly wrenched by the crash landing. Recovering his wits quickly, however, Campbell immediately decided to make the return run over the course. In an interview later, he said that if he had stepped out of the Bluebird after the mishap, he would not have been able to force himself back into the driver's seat.

After a quick check of the Bluebird by the crew, no damage

In 1928 Malcolm Campbell drove this Bluebird racer to a record speed of 206.96 miles per hour.

THE BRITISH PETROLEUM CO., LTD.

was found. The English sportsman drove his Bluebird down the beach for several miles and then swung it around and pointed toward the measured mile course. This time Campbell was lucky and had no mishaps. The wind, however, hindered his speed and he could not push the Bluebird past the 200-mile mark. Nevertheless, when Campbell's times for the two speed runs over the course were averaged, he had reclaimed the world record with a new high of 206.95 miles per hour.

Although happy to have regained the speed crown, Captain Campbell was not completely satisfied with his triumph. He wished the new record had been set at a higher mark, not so close to Segrave's old record. Campbell would have preferred to put the world speed record further out of reach of the two American drivers who were about to follow him onto the sands of Daytona Beach.

Chapter 5
A British-American Speed Duel

Frank Lockhart and Ray Keech were two rough-and-tumble, experienced racing car drivers. They had spent countless hours behind the wheels of high-speed automobiles on tracks throughout the United States. Lockhart was the more famous of the two, mainly because of his sensational driving in the Indianapolis Speedway Races, the nation's best-known motor car competition.

Both drivers had come to Daytona Beach in February of 1928 with their high-powered automobiles, determined to make their contributions to the steady quest for speed and more speed. Their arrival marked the beginning of an unofficial duel between British and American drivers for the world automobile speed record.

Frank Lockhart lived and breathed only for automobiles. While still in knee pants he had worked in garages as an apprentice mechanic. He had quickly learned everything there was to know about automobiles, especially how to make them go at top speed. Then Lockhart had his first opportunity to drive a high-speed motor car in a track race and from that moment on his life's ambition was to be a racing car driver.

Over the next several years Lockhart roared to victory after victory on all the major racing car tracks in California. His fame as a daring, skillful driver soon spread beyond the borders of his home state, and he turned his attention to the famous Indianapolis 500.

After a series of sensational triumphs on the Indianapolis track and elsewhere in the country, Frank Lockhart decided to give up this kind of competition. He began to concentrate on the challenge of building and racing automobiles to attain the highest speed possible. He read about the exploits of Captain Malcolm Campbell and Major Henry O. Segrave and their magnificent racing cars, and dreamed of holding the world automobile speed crown himself.

As Campbell and Segrave so well realized, it took a great deal of money to build and operate an automobile that could go faster than any other in the world. Lockhart overcame this financial problem by enlisting the help of auto manufacturers and tire and oil companies. In return for their assistance, these companies would receive valuable advertising from Lockhart's use of their products. With finances taken care of, the next question was what kind of automobile to use for the speed record attempt.

The years Lockhart had spent tinkering with the engines of racing cars to coax the last ounce of power from them, and the equally long years he had spent driving these vehicles, had left him with definite ideas on what his record-seeking automobile should be like. Of one thing he was certain: the car would not be a giant like the British juggernauts.

Frank Lockhart thought in terms of a medium-size automobile, highly streamlined and propelled by a very powerful engine. The vehicle would not weigh much more than a ton and a half. The youthful speedster found sympathetic listeners at the Stutz motor car company, the builder of a very popular automobile for the general public in the 1920s.

Stutz automotive engineers and Lockhart put their heads to-

Frank Lockhart in a Miller Special that he drove to victory in the Indianapolis 500 of 1926.

INDIANAPOLIS MOTOR SPEEDWAY OFFICIAL PHOTOS

gether and worked for months over drafting boards and in machine shops. Finally, the dream car was completed and rolled from the factory. It was called the Stutz Black Hawk, a trim, white beauty powered by two Miller engines combined into a single power unit of sixteen cylinders. Miller engines were the most famous American-made engines at the time for powering racing cars.

The Stutz Black Hawk came close to the standards set by Frank Lockhart. The car was small as he had wanted, weighing slightly over 2800 pounds. The specially built Miller engine produced 570 horsepower—enough, so the creators of the car believed, to propel it at more than 200 miles per hour. The wheels were shrouded in streamlined covers to reduce wind resistance. The car's body was narrow and tapered at the front and back. Compared to the monsters driven by Segrave and Campbell, Lockhart's machine was a pygmy.

Frank Lockhart arrived at Daytona Beach with his Stutz Black Hawk in the winter of 1928, in time for Speed Week. Captain Campbell was already there with his magnificent Bluebird, so the young racing car driver had ample opportunity to watch a veteran speedster perform.

The important job for Lockhart, however, was to find out as quickly as he could how the Stutz Black Hawk behaved at high speeds. His first test run was a disappointment. Try as Lockhart would, he just could not get the vehicle to go faster than 180 miles per hour. This might have been swift enough for other kinds of automobile competition, but not for breaking the world speed record.

Working with almost frantic haste, Lockhart and his crew of mechanics finally located the problem. Air was not flowing properly into the engine's superchargers. When this was remedied, the graceful little racer performed more to Lockhart's satisfaction. Now he was ready for the big test.

Campbell had set a new world land speed record on February 19. Three days later Frank Lockhart announced that he would try to top the Englishman's mark of 206.96 miles per hour. The weather continued dreadful on the day Lockhart planned to make his run, as rainy, windy, and cold as it had been for Captain Campbell.

Lockhart's crew tried to persuade him to postpone his speed run until the weather improved. But Lockhart refused. He was eager to put his speedy automobile to its big test. Besides, he felt a certain obligation to the crowds of spectators who had paid a grandstand admission fee to watch his performance.

It was late afternoon when Lockhart came to the beach with his Stutz Black Hawk. In what his crew considered an omen of good luck, the rain had stopped; the clouds parted and the sun came out. Following the standard procedure for the flying mile run, Lockhart and his sleek, white car were towed several miles down the beach from the starting line. He intended to arrive at the start of the measured mile moving as close to top speed as possible.

As his crew stepped away from the car, Lockhart started the engine. There was a loud, ear-shattering whine. The noise increased in intensity as Lockhart opened the throttle wider. He released the brakes and the slim racing car began to roll, slowly at first and then, in seconds, faster and faster. By the time Lockhart reached the starting flags, almost opposite the grandstand, he was streaking at nearly 200 miles per hour.

Lockhart unleashed all the power his swift Black Hawk possessed. In a twinkling, before any of the onlookers were aware, Lockhart and his racing car were no longer moving in a straight line. Instead, car and driver were bounding end over end across the beach. With a mighty splash, the vehicle landed in the surf, luckily in an upright position. The initial momentum, however, kept the car moving across the top of the water, like a stone skimming over the crest of the waves. Finally it stopped and settled in the water which nearly covered both driver and car.

No one thought Lockhart had survived the crash. But suddenly his arm shot into the air as he began to wave. His crew and many of the spectators dashed to his rescue. They hauled him out of the vehicle, in which he had become wedged, and carried him to the beach.

Except for shock and some minor cuts, Lockhart came out of the accident in good shape. Amazingly, even the Stutz Black

Hawk had not suffered too badly. However, it definitely needed repairs, so the youthful driver left Daytona with his racer to fix the damage and to get some needed rest himself.

Frank Lockhart's disastrous run did not end the attempts to break the world's automobile speed record during Speed Week. Ray Keech had his turn next. Keech had lots of fast-car experience. He had been a professional racing car driver for a number of years, roaring around many of the best-known race tracks in the country. Although he was not as famous as Lockhart, Keech had proved himself a skilled and daring driver.

Ray Keech acquired his high-speed driving skill on race tracks throughout the country. This picture shows Keech in the racer with which he won the Indianapolis 500 of 1929.

THE FIRESTONE TIRE & RUBBER COMPANY

Ray Keech in the driver's seat of the White Triplex, in which he attempted to set a new world speed record in April, 1928. Note the double set of rear wheels needed to carry the great weight of the twin rear engines.

INDIANAPOLIS MOTOR SPEEDWAY OFFICIAL PHOTOS

Keech had come to Daytona with a four-wheeled juggernaut called the White Triplex. The car was named for J. H. White, an automobile enthusiast and sportsman from Philadelphia, who had financed the Triplex's construction as well as its trip to Florida.

The Triplex was a mammoth, powerful machine. Tipping the scales at four tons, it was in the same weight class as the record-shattering British speedsters. Keech's racer was unique in that it was powered by three enormous Liberty aircraft engines. These had become famous in World War I for propelling American training and fighter planes. On the Triplex, one engine was placed in front of the driver and two were located at the rear.

The builders of the Triplex scarcely bothered to streamline the monster car. Their plan was to smash through to a new speed record with sheer brute power.

The day after Lockhart's accident, Keech brought the mammoth Triplex to the beach and prepared for his speed run. After a few minor adjustments by his mechanics, Keech started the engines. Their roar and thunder could be heard hundreds of feet away. Then he shifted into gear and began to roll—but not far. A hose in the cooling system of one of the engines suddenly exploded, and a geyser of scalding hot water showered over the driver and car. Fortunately, Keech escaped serious injury, but the mishap put an end to any speed runs for the day.

Repairs took longer than expected and it was mid-April before Keech returned to the beach with the White Triplex. This time his speed run went according to plan. He boomed over the sand with an ear-shattering roar, first in one direction and then in the opposite. When the timers averaged the speeds for the American driver's two runs, they announced that he had set a new automobile land speed mark of 207.55 miles per hour. To be sure, this was only a hairsbreadth over Captain Campbell's record of

This picture shows the White Triplex without its double set of rear wheels.   THE BRITISH PETROLEUM CO., LTD.

206.96 miles per hour. Nevertheless, it was a higher speed and certainly good enough for Ray Keech and the record book.

In the meantime, Frank Lockhart was repairing his Stutz Black Hawk with all possible speed. He was anxious to return to Daytona Beach and make his speed run before Keech, if possible. When he heard the news of what his American rival had done, Lockhart was disappointed. He decided to make his own speed record attempt anyway, determined now to take the crown away from Ray Keech.

By the middle of April Lockhart was again at Daytona with his Stutz Black Hawk. Both he and his slim racer were once more in first-class condition. Indeed, some changes had been made to the Black Hawk's engine so the car was considered even faster than before.

Early on the morning of April 25, Frank Lockhart took his sleek, swift automobile to the beach and made ready for the attack on Keech's record. Timekeepers were posted at the required positions on the measured mile.

Sitting quietly and confidently in the cockpit of his trim racer some distance from the starting flags, Lockhart warmed up the engine. He listened with an expert's ear for the slightest sound that might signal trouble. But the machine rumbled rhythmically and, at a signal from the starter, the young driver released the brakes and shot forward toward the starting line. Moving with the speed of an arrow in flight, Lockhart covered the mile at a good rate. After flashing over the finish line he slowed his speed, turned the Black Hawk around, and sped back to the original starting point.

Frank Lockhart was keenly disappointed to hear that his two runs were not good enough for a new record. Without leaving the cockpit of his car, he headed the vehicle over the course for another try. This time he pressed his foot even harder on the accelerator. His white racer hummed as it streaked beautifully over the sandy course under the steady, skillful hand of the young driver.

In the middle of his return run, traveling at full throttle, Lockhart and his Stutz Black Hawk suddenly began to plunge wildly end over end across the beach. Before the spectators' horrified eyes, the vehicle bounded into the air, crunched into the sand with a thud, then bounded into the air again. It crashed back onto the beach upside down, a crumpled wreck. Frank Lockhart, not

The highly streamlined Stutz Black Hawk in which Frank Lockhart made his fatal attempt to set a new world speed record. The auto was sometimes called the Stutz-Lockhart because Lockhart contributed so many ideas to its design and construction.

INDIANAPOLIS MOTOR SPEEDWAY OFFICIAL PHOTOS

Daytona Beach Florida February 1928.

Stutz-Lockhart Race Car

so fortunate this time, was seriously injured; he was rushed to a hospital but died soon after arriving.

Lockhart's crew and the officials timing the test run concluded that a tire blowout had caused the accident. Perhaps cut by the sharp edge of a clamshell, the blown tire had made the Black Hawk completely unmanageable.

More than thirty years were to pass before American drivers followed Frank Lockhart and Ray Keech and again challenged the British.

Chapter 6
New Glory for
British Speedsters

Even after the tragedy in 1928, the quest for still higher automobile speed records continued unabated. Throughout the 1930s the world auto speed mark was steadily raised, mainly by British drivers.

Major Henry Segrave and Captain Malcolm Campbell lost little time in putting the upstart American drivers in their place in the automobile speed record game. Segrave reached Daytona Beach first with a brand-new, magnificently designed and built speedster, the Golden Arrow. The vehicle proved just as magnificent in performance. On March 11, 1929, Segrave scorched the Daytona sands with a new world speed mark of 231.44 miles per hour, shattering Keech's old record by more than 24 miles per hour. There was no doubt who the auto speed king was now.

Campbell extended warm congratulations to Segrave for a splendid speed run, and then began building a new and more powerful Bluebird. He was determined to outperform his countryman.

When finished, the new Bluebird was a dazzling sight. Every line of its gracefully contoured blue body expressed surging

The Golden Arrow driven by Henry Segrave in 1929 to a world record speed of 231.44 miles per hour.

power and swiftness. Beneath an incredibly long front hood was an aircraft engine, a Napier twelve-cylinder power unit that could generate more than 1400 horsepower.

On February 5, 1931, hunched low in the driver's seat and clutching the wheel firmly with both hands, Campbell roared over the course at Daytona Beach to a new world speed mark of 246.09 miles per hour. He had beaten his arch rival Segrave by a comfortable margin of more than fifteen miles per hour.

Captain Campbell's new record was his fifth in a long, brilliant series of successes that had begun in 1925. His fame as a daring driver of super-fast automobiles had spread throughout the world. But the loudest plaudits came from his native England. Returning home after his 1931 achievement, Campbell was looked upon as a national hero. For his daring accomplishments and the honor he had brought to Great Britain, Captain Malcolm Campbell was knighted by King George V.

In his years of driving lightning-swift automobiles to one world speed record after another, Captain Campbell had acquired enough honors to satisfy the average racing car driver. Campbell was already in his mid-forties at the time of his 1931 triumph but he was not yet ready to quit. He had a secret ambition, known to only a few close friends, which he hoped to achieve before giving up the sport. This was to crack the 300 miles per hour barrier. His 1931 speed record did not leave too much more to go and Campbell felt strongly that with further engineering refinements, his beloved Bluebird could do it.

Slowly but steadily, the fearless British racing car driver raised the world land speed mark toward the 300-mile goal. In 1932 he boosted the figure to more than 253 miles per hour. The following year Campell did even better with a big increase to 272 miles per hour. In order to reach that sizzling pace, Captain Campbell had the old Napier engine removed from the Bluebird and replaced with a more powerful twelve-cylinder Rolls-Royce airplane engine. This remarkable engine had powered swift British Schneider Cup racing seaplanes to speeds of more than 340 miles per hour.

Campbell's speed run of 1933 was his last for nearly two years. During this time he and his engineers drastically rebuilt the Bluebird in an effort to give the sleek machine more speed than ever before.

Malcolm Campbell's Napier-Bluebird of 1932, in which he set a new world speed record of 253.97 miles per hour.

THE BRITISH PETROLEUM CO., LTD.

Two striking changes were evident in the rebuilt Bluebird when it appeared in 1935. Most unusual, perhaps, were the racing car's twin rear wheels. Instead of two wheels as before, four wheels now propelled the vehicle. It was felt that the extra wheels would give the car better traction while traveling at top speed.

The front end of the racer's body had also been changed. Whereas the front had been slightly tapered, it now had a broad, sloping shape like a wedge. A narrow slot opening along the front edge of this broad nose permitted air to enter and help cool the engine.

There were mechanical changes too that could not be seen unless the car's body shell was removed. A new front axle had been installed as well as an improved restraint system for the driver's protection. A novel feature of the new Bluebird was a set of air brakes to help the vehicle's mechanical brakes. The air brakes were movable panels located on the upper portion of fenderlike extensions directly behind the rear wheels. The panels could be raised to a near vertical position by a driver-operated mechanism. The onrushing air stream pressing against the panels would resist the vehicle's forward progress and help to slow it down.

In March of 1935 Campbell brought his new Bluebird to Daytona Beach in high hopes of shattering the 300 miles per hour barrier. Winter weather had left the beach very rough. Nevertheless, Campbell took his ponderous thunderbolt, which weighed more than five tons, to the sandy measured stretch of beach and made the required two runs. The best he could do was a disappointing 276-plus miles per hour.

Campbell and his colleagues had not worked on the Bluebird for two years just to beat the world speed record by a mere four miles per hour. He was certain the car could do better. However, Campbell decided that before another speed attempt was made, a new course had to be found. Daytona Beach was no longer suitable.

Aside from the rough and soft spots on the sandy beach, which could easily throw an automobile traveling at bullet speed out of control, the course was no longer of sufficient length. For a vehicle capable of speeds close to 300 miles per hour, there was not enough room to accelerate to top speed for the approach to the starting line, nor enough room to slow down after passing the finish marker. Voicing his criticisms of Daytona Beach to racing acquaintances in the United States, Captain Campbell was told to consider the Bonneville Salt Flats in northwest Utah.

The geological remains of a vast inland sea, the Bonneville Salt Flats are an enormous level desertlike stretch of coarse salt. Without an obstruction to break its expanse, distance on the flats is so great that one can actually see the horizon bend to the earth's curvature. Named for an early nineteenth-century American explorer of the west, Lieutenant George Bonneville, the flats had been used by racing car drivers for many years but not on the scale of Daytona Beach. When Campbell came to the Bonneville Salt Flats in the late summer of 1935 with his Bluebird, he saw immediately that here was all the space he needed.

On September 3, Campbell and his Bluebird were ready for another try at cracking the 300 miles per hour barrier. A stretch of salt more than ten miles long was smoothed out for the record run attempt. A broad black stripe of oil was brushed down the middle of the course; this was to be Campbell's guide as he whizzed over the course at lightning speed. After a brief trial run to get the feel of the new terrain, Campbell was ready for the big test. Pleased by what he had found, the British sportsman knew that if the Bluebird had the power to travel 300 miles per hour or better, this was the place to prove it.

Squeezing the last ounce of power from the mighty Rolls-Royce engine, Captain Campbell and his beloved Bluebird finally accomplished what no other driver or racing car had done before— zipping over the earth's surface at a speed of more than 300 miles

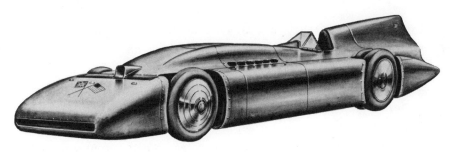

Powered by Rolls-Royce engines, Malcolm Campbell's beautifully designed Bluebird achieved a new world speed record of 301.13 miles per hour on September 3, 1935. This was Campbell's first experience on the Bonneville Salt Flats.

THE BRITISH PETROLEUM CO., LTD.

per hour. Campbell's exact time was 301.13 miles per hour. Not many in the automotive world had believed that this speed could ever be achieved by a landbound vehicle. For Captain Campbell it was quite a triumph personally. He had accomplished the feat at the age of fifty, a time when most drivers of racing cars were content to sit in a rocking chair talking of past glories instead of in the cockpit of a super-swift automobile.

Captain Malcolm Campbell's achievement at Bonneville Salt Flats ended his career as a seeker of land speed records. He was content to have reached his goal of passing 300 miles per hour; others could now take up where he had left off.

And there were others who were willing to try. Indeed, just two years after Campbell's retirement, two of these challenging daredevils made an appearance. Like Campbell, Captain George Eyston and John Cobb were British.

Captain Eyston was a popular racing car driver who had captured many prizes on tracks in England and Europe. John Cobb had also acquired a love for fast cars in racing competition. In the late 1930s, just before the outbreak of World War II, these two speedsters carried on a duel for the world's automobile speed crown that was every bit as spirited as the one between Major Segrave and Captain Campbell. Eyston was the first to throw down the gauntlet with a huge machine called the Thunderbolt.

Superbly engineered and highly streamlined, the massive auto tipped the scales at almost seven tons. It was powered by a pair of Rolls-Royce aircraft engines whose combined output was close to 5000 horsepower. The engines were placed side by side in the middle of the Thunderbolt's body and, through a complex mechanical arrangement, transmitted their enormous power to the racer's rear wheels. The driver sat in front of this rumbling powerhouse.

The Thunderbolt rolled on eight wheels—four in front and four in back. The front wheel arrangement was unique in that each pair of wheels was placed one in front of the other. The first wheel was narrower than the one directly behind it, so that the car's front end could be tapered for a sharper streamlined effect. Both pairs of front wheels could be steered by the driver.

The four back wheels were simply twin wheels placed side by side, similar to the arrangement pioneered by Captain Campbell on one of his Bluebirds.

Another feature that was similar to several of the Bluebirds was the large vertical fin on the Thunderbolt's tail end. This was to help the driver maintain better directional control of the racer while traveling at top speed. The body of the Thunderbolt, smooth and sleek, was made of aluminum and was painted silver.

Captain Eyston and his shiny Thunderbolt came to Bonneville Salt Flats in the early fall of 1937. By this time the flats were considered the only safe and practical place to unleash the full power of high-speed vehicles. The English speedster planned to make his run in early October; by the end of that month turbulent winter weather was likely to put an end to record speed efforts for another year.

A series of unexpected storms and mechanical breakdowns frustrated Eyston's assault on Campbell's record. However, during this period Eyston had been able to make several test drives with the Thunderbolt at speeds of more than 300 miles per hour. He felt certain that the Thunderbolt had the power and speed to surpass Campbell's old mark.

After a nerve-wracking wait for repairs, Eyston and his speedy silver bullet were finally ready for the big test by mid-November. Time was running out for the English sportsman since winter was due to arrive on the flats any day. The measured mile course with its black oil stripe had been prepared and scraped smooth days earlier.

A starting car, pushing against the rear of the Thunderbolt, got Eyston moving several miles from the starting line. This procedure was used to reduce the strain which starting up produced on the Thunderbolt's complicated gears. Eyston zoomed over the starting line with his engine rumbling at full power. He shot out of view of the small group of spectators in seconds. But when the officials announced the time of the first run—slightly more than 305 miles per hour—Eyston was far from satisfied. He knew the Thunderbolt could go a lot faster, and he would prove this to himself and the onlookers on the run back.

New tires were placed on all eight wheels of the Thunderbolt. The racer was refueled and within minutes Eyston was ready for the second dash. According to the international rules, a driver had to make a second run within an hour after the completion of the first. Eyston's crew worked like a well-drilled team so there was more than ample time.

Once again Captain Eyston and his silver Thunderbolt flashed over the starting line. His foot pressed the accelerator harder than ever. To the onlookers he was not much more than a blur on the desolate landscape. This time the news was better. He had hit a top speed of 319 miles per hour. When this was averaged with

This is Captain George Eyston's powerful Thunderbolt with which he twice cracked the world land speed record.

his speed on the first run, Captain Eyston had taken the world's land speed crown from Malcolm Campbell. The new record was 312.00 miles per hour.

Pleased with his triumph, Captain Eyston left the Bonneville Salt Flats with his Thunderbolt to return to his home in England. He planned to come back to America in the fall of 1938, confident that he and his mighty Thunderbolt could push the world automobile speed mark even higher. However, when Eyston returned to the Salt Flats speed arena, he discovered that he was not to have the course to himself. A fellow countryman, John Cobb, was also present with a super-swift automobile and with plans of his own for setting a new motor car speed record.

Cobb was a big man, soft-spoken and wholly without nerves when it came to driving automobiles at breakneck speeds. For years he had been a top-notch driver on auto tracks and in cross-country racing. Then he had turned his thoughts to capturing the world's automobile speed crown. To build his highly specialized super-racer, Cobb had engaged Reid A. Railton.

Railton was a genius at designing and building lightning-swift automobiles. He had created many of Captain Campbell's record-breaking Bluebirds. Cobb gave Railton a free hand and the talented automotive engineer did not fail in his assignment. The motor car that eventually emerged was both beautiful to look at and incredibly swift. In honor of its creator, the machine was called the Railton.

Cobb's new racer had many imaginative engineering features. Railton believed as Frank Lockhart had that the fastest automobile in the world need not be a ponderous juggernaut. He kept the weight of Cobb's racer to about three tons as contrasted with the seven tons of Eyston's Thunderbolt. Two Napier aircraft engines, improved versions of the kind in Campbell's Bluebirds, powered the Railton. These produced a combined output of 1250 horsepower.

Railton installed the twin engines in an ingenious way. Rather than placing them side by side, he staggered the units, one slightly ahead of the other. Thus he was able to keep the racer's body reasonably narrow. The forward engine was geared to drive the front wheels, and the rear power unit drove the rear wheels. This arrangement was also novel for super-fast automobiles. Although only half the weight of the giant Thunderbolt, Cobb's Railton was no midget as racing cars went. It was nearly thirty feet long and almost eight feet wide.

In the blazing heat of late August, the two British daredevils prepared to square off for their speed duel. Captain George Eyston was to go first with his reworked Thunderbolt. The measured course was again scraped smooth and marked with a black guide-line. Electronic eyes and time recorders were now used at the start and finish of the mile course.

On August 27 Eyston wheeled his huge machine out on the flats and unleashed the power of its mighty engines. With John Cobb among the absorbed spectators, Eyston made two superlative runs over the course for an average speed and a new record of 345.50 miles per hour. His mighty Thunderbolt had indeed showed far more "thunder" than in the previous year.

The new world auto speed record established by Eyston was a formidable mark. But after the usual congratulations, John Cobb went quietly to work with his Railton. After some trial runs and minor mechanical adjustments, Cobb was ready to try for the record on September 15.

Cobb squeezed his huge body behind the wheel of the tear-drop-shaped Railton and rolled to a point several miles from the starting line. He gunned the engines to an ear-shattering roar and in seconds was moving along the course like a bullet. His top speed on the way out was a dazzling 353.2 miles per hour. Cobb's return dash was somewhat slower, 347.2 miles per hour. But the average of the two speeds was enough to make John Cobb the new speed king of the automotive world. The record now stood at 350.20 miles per hour.

The speed duel between the two Englishmen was now on in earnest. Eyston had made a few changes on his Thunderbolt, mostly to improve the streamlining. The biggest job was the removal of the vertical fin from the tail end. Eyston no longer believed that this feature was needed for controlling the directional path of his racer. In fact, he considered it a hindrance, acting as a drag while the car moved at top speed.

On the morning after Cobb's record drive, Eyston was back on the measured mile course with his Thunderbolt. He streaked back and forth over the flats for an average speed of 357.50 miles per

Shaped like a teardrop, the highly streamlined Railton was driven by John Cobb to three world speed records. The first was 350.20 miles per hour on September 15, 1938.

THE BRITISH PETROLEUM CO., LTD.

hour. Once again he was king of the world's automobile speed-sters.

Both drivers called it quits after that and returned to England. Although disappointed that his record had lasted for such a brief time, Cobb was convinced that his sleek Railton had hardly been extended. Under its beautifully streamlined body was a great deal more power and speed. Like Campbell aiming for 300 miles per hour, John Cobb was determined to be the first driver of a motor car to crash the 400-mile speed barrier.

Through the winter of 1938-1939, John Cobb, Reid Railton, and their crew of mechanics worked on the super-racer. The changes they made were all designed to add still greater speed to this earthbound streak of lightning. By late August of 1939, Cobb and his Railton were once again in the United States, zooming over the Bonneville Salt Flats.

The changes Cobb and his colleagues had made proved to be

the right ones. The Englishman regained the world speed crown by flashing over the flats for an average speed of 369.70 miles per hour. But try as he would, Cobb could not push the Railton closer to the 400-mile mark.

World War II broke out while John Cobb was still in the United States and ended any further attempts to break the world automobile speed record. Captain George Eyston had remained in England and, in fact, never again took part in these hazardous speed activities. John Cobb stored his precious Railton for the duration of the war. He hoped to continue his quest for speed and more speed when peace returned to a troubled world.

After the war, Cobb lost little time in returning to his first love—driving the world's fastest motor car. The Railton was taken out of storage and plans made for new assaults on the world land speed record. Both Cobb and Reid Railton felt the racer needed only a few changes to make it ready for new speed runs. Since it had now become enormously expensive to build, maintain, and operate the world's fastest automobile, Cobb sought financial backing for his speed ambitions. The Mobil Oil Company came to his aid, and in exchange, Cobb agreed to carry the company's name on his racer. It now became the Railton-Mobil Special.

It was not easy in the immediate postwar years to find necessary parts, equipment, or even skilled mechanics to work on the Railton. After months of frustrating activity, John Cobb finally arrived at the scene of his prewar triumphs, the Bonneville Salt Flats, in August of 1947. The British sportsman and his crew of mechanics worked quickly to get the racer ready for trial runs before the big test.

After the last of several test spins on the flats, Cobb came back to his waiting crew with an unhappy expression on his face. The powerful engines of his racer were not throbbing smoothly. The mechanics plunged into the depths of the engines with wrenches and screwdrivers to find the cause of the problem. The offending parts were discovered and removed. It was quickly decided by all that these had to be replaced. This meant sending all the way to England for new parts—a long and trying wait for John Cobb and his crew.

The replacements came at last and soon the engines sounded their more normal thunderous rhythm. But Cobb still could not make his much desired final run. This time the weather intervened. As the last weeks of summer gave way to autumn, strong, gusting winds swept across the flats, making high-speed driving out of the question. The winds would not only retard the speed of the racer but might also send it out of control.

It was September 14 when John Cobb and his crew finally got the Railton-Mobil Special out on the flats and ready to roll. He shot through the first half of his run at the modest speed of a little more than 375 miles per hour. Alas, there was to be no second run that day. The course was not in the smoothest condition and Cobb's rough ride had caused portions of the racer to fall off. So it was back to the shed for repairs and a delay of two more days. The crew worked as rapidly as possible; with winter fast approaching, the time for high-speed runs on the flats was slipping away.

On September 16 Cobb was once again on the flats, squeezed into the tiny driver's compartment of his powerful racer. The streamlined hood was lowered over his head, the safety harness hooked in place, and Cobb was ready to go.

A small truck eased up to the tail of the Railton and gently pushed it forward. The engines churned into life accompanied by puffs of black smoke. Cobb pressed his foot on the accelerator and the engines responded with a throbbing rumbling roar. The silver racer began to roll, slowly at first, then faster and faster. Cobb had about six miles in which to accelerate his vehicle to near maximum speed before coming to the start of the measured mile.

The Railton was streaking like a silver bullet as the starting marker loomed ahead. Cobb's foot pressed still more firmly on the fuel pedal. He took his eyes off the black guide stripe for a split second to glance at the speedometer. The indicator needle had slowly eased past the 400 figure and was moving higher! "Success at last!" flashed through Cobb's mind. He was moving at a lightning rate, if only for mere seconds, that many in the automotive world had thought technically impossible.

But, though Cobb's speedometer indicated that he had reached and exceeded 400 miles per hour, the official timers had recorded his super-fast journey at a little more than 385 miles per hour. It was a good mark and if he could repeat it on his second run back, he would surely smash his old record of 369 miles per hour. But Cobb wanted to do more than that. The figure of 400 miles per hour still haunted him.

After a quick engine check by the crew, a fresh supply of fuel poured into the tanks, and new tires put on the wheels, Cobb pointed his Railton-Mobil Special for home. He crossed the start of the measured mile like a silver blur. Cobb pressed the accelerator all the way down as he hurtled over the salt surface. Within seconds he shot across the finish marker and headed off into the distance before he could bring his powerful racer to a stop.

Getting back to the official timers as quickly as he could, Cobb was anxious to hear the results. His return trip had certainly been a sensational effort—just over 403 miles per hour! He had covered the mile-long course in less than nine seconds! When this was averaged with his speed for the first run, Cobb's new world land speed record for automobiles was 394.20 miles per hour.

This was not 400 miles per hour and John Cobb felt a measure of disappointment. The daring driver, however, had to be content with the fact that he and his Railton-Mobil Special had done the best they could. His new record was a formidable mark and it

The Railton-Mobil Special driven by John Cobb to a new world land speed record of 394.20 miles per hour in 1947.

proved to be John Cobb's swan song. He never again sat behind the wheel of a super-racer.

The mark set by John Cobb in 1947 remained on the record books for sixteen years. Anyone with ambitions to surpass the Englishman's accomplishment realized that it would require a super-machine. After almost two decades of inactivity, a new family of incredibly swift, ultramodern automobiles appeared to challenge Cobb's achievement. These super-fast, magnificent machines and their fearless drivers opened an entirely new era in the endless pursuit of speed and more speed.

Chapter 7
The Big Boomers

The year was 1963. Craig Breedlove sat hunched in the driver's seat of his Spirit of America. A red and white crash helmet was fixed firmly to his head. The Plexiglas canopy overhead was pulled tight. The heat within the enclosed cockpit, under a scorching August sun, was intense. Although it was still early in the morning, temperatures on the Bonneville Salt Flats rise quickly under a cloudless sky.

But the youthful driver was totally unaware of any physical discomfort. The dream of a lifetime was about to be fulfilled as he attempted to drive the fastest automobile in the world. Would he succeed? Or would the years of planning and hard work, and the spending of his last dollar in developing his big boomer, end in failure? Within a few minutes Craig Breedlove would have his answer.

The big boomers, of which Craig Breedlove's Spirit of America was the first, were fantastic machines that owed their existence to the flood of technological advances of World War II and the immediate postwar period. Two of the most startling of these technical developments were the turbojet and rocket engines. These revolutionary power units had been harnessed to airplanes and unmanned aerial missiles, propelling them at super-speeds. Before the war these fantastic velocities would have been considered possible only in the realm of science fiction.

Almost two decades after John Cobb's record-breaking dash, daring young racing car drivers were ready to mate the tremendously powerful turbojet and rocket engines to the automobile. Thus the big boomers, incredibly swift jet- and rocket-powered racing cars, were born.

Craig Breedlove was a young Californian who had fallen in love with automobiles at an early age. He particularly loved cars that could travel at super-speeds. Inevitably he became attracted to auto racing. He developed into an expert at drag strip racing with a reputation throughout California.

But Breedlove had far more important ambitions which he spoke about only rarely to a few close friends. He dreamed that one day he would own and drive the fastest motor vehicle in the world. Breedlove was familiar with the achievements of the motor car speed kings of the past and was determined to outperform them.

Drag strip racing and many first-place finishes eventually gave the young driver the necessary financial means to launch his project in the early 1960s. Thereafter all his thoughts and activities were centered on the creation of his super-swift dream car. He knew exactly what kind of car he wanted and went about building it in a thoroughly professional way.

For example, Breedlove wanted a turbojet engine to power his racer. He knew this would be superior to the most advanced automobile piston engine for pushing his car into the ultrahigh speed range he was aiming for. The car would be propelled forward by the simple thrust action—or more correctly, reaction—of the engines, just as a jet-powered aircraft or a rocket-driven missile is propelled.

With the help of an aeronautical engineer friend, Breedlove then designed a super-streamlined body to house the powerful engine. They first worked out the shape for the racer's body with the help of a model. This was taken to a wind tunnel where, in powerful mechanically-made currents of air, the body design was thoroughly tested. The same procedure is used when a new airplane wing or fuselage is created and tested.

After Breedlove and his friend were satisfied that their design had the least possible wind resistance, or drag, actual construction of the dream racer began. The workshop was a garage in Breedlove's backyard. Very early in the project, the young driver named his big boomer the Spirit of America.

Craig Breedlove soon came up against the problem common to many earlier builders of super-fast motor cars—money. If his automobile was ever to be finished and tested on the salt flats, Breedlove would need much more money than his personal finances could provide. He was forced to suspend construction and go on a sales campaign to enlist financial support for his project.

Brimming with enthusiasm and confidence, Breedlove made the rounds of oil companies and automobile tire manufacturers, whose products could be used for his automobile. In return for their financial help, the companies would gain valuable advertising from the publicity of Breedlove's record speed attempt—especially if he were successful. The sincerity and spirit of the young driver won the day. Shell Oil and the Goodyear Tire and Rubber Company agreed to provide Breedlove with the necessary money not only to complete his automobile but to make the test runs on the flats.

One day in the spring of 1962, Craig Breedlove and his small group of fellow workers stepped back to admire their finished handiwork. Gleaming in its blue and white paint, the automobile was striking in appearance. If it ran as well as it looked, they would all be happy, feeling that their countless hours of labor had not been in vain.

Craig Breedlove and his super-fast Spirit of America.

By any standards of the automotive world Craig Breedlove's dream car was an unusual vehicle. Its pencil-slim body, thirty-five feet from nose to tail, had only three wheels. Two were at the rear of the body and were mounted on an eleven-foot-wide axle. The third wheel was beneath the tapered nose section. This was a fixed wheel that could not be turned to the right or left for steering purposes.

Directly in front of the nose wheel was a downward-pointing vertical fin. On an airplane this would be called a canard fin and would help stabilize the aircraft's directional flight at high speeds. In addition to acting as a directional stabilizer on the

Spirit of America, the canard fin was movable and helped to steer the vehicle, much like a boat's rudder. Breedlove could also steer his racer by locking either the right or left rear wheel, making the car pivot around the locked wheel. However, early test runs showed that this original steering arrangement left much to be desired. The front wheel was therefore changed so the driver could turn it to the right or left.

Both the front wheel and the two back wheels were concealed within highly streamlined shields. The axle connecting the two rear wheels was also enclosed within a streamlined covering. Viewed from above, the axle shroud looked like the stubby wings of an airplane. Indeed, the Spirit of America's close relation to the design of an airplane could be seen from any angle. This impression was further enhanced by a towering six-foot vertical fin attached to the car's tail end. As on an airplane, the purpose of the fin was to help the driver keep the machine pointed in a straight line while moving at top speed.

Two elongated bulges, beginning at a point near the enclosed cockpit and extending rearward, were located one on each side of the car's body. Openings at their front ends funneled the necessary torrents of air to the turbojet engine as the car sped forward.

The powerful engine was buried within the body of the super-swift racer, just to the rear of the driver's cockpit. Its scorching hot exhaust gases rushed out of the tail opening with a tremendous roar. The engine that Breedlove managed to get hold of for his racer was a J-47 turbojet. It was a popular type of the time, used in some of the fastest fighter planes in the United States Air Force, such as the F-104.

Poised on its three wheels, the Spirit of America looked like some strange mechanical bird that had just alighted on the ground. Every line of the car's structure denoted grace and swiftness. And yet the racer was no lightweight. It tipped the scales at three tons.

It was one thing to create an automobile that could speed at better than 400 miles per hour. It was something else to think of an efficient way to bring such a machine to a halt. For an effective braking system, Breedlove borrowed again from the aviation world: he installed a parachute system in the tail section of his car. When a driver traveling at top speed wanted to stop the racer, he would press a button to pop two parachutes from a compartment. Fully opened and dragging at the rear, the 'chutes would help to slow the vehicle to a manageable speed, at which point the car's conventional brakes on the rear wheels could be applied. The parachute braking system was originally developed to help slow speedy military jet planes during landings.

Finally, in August of 1963, Breedlove and the Spirit of America waited in the shimmering heat of the Bonneville Salt Flats. The graceful car shook gently with the surging rumbling power of its turbojet engine. Breedlove ran his eyes and hand over the gauges and controls in a last-minute check. Then his hand shot up in a signal. Crewmen ran to the rear wheels and removed the wooden blocks. They stood back expectantly as Breedlove opened the throttle. He released the brakes and the machine began to roll.

The Spirit of America moved slowly at first, then quickly picked up momentum. Breedlove pointed straight for the black guide stripe on the measured mile. The starting markers were almost three miles away. In seconds the young driver shot over the starting line. A few seconds more and he was through the course and into the slow-down stretch.

To slow the swift Spirit of America, Breedlove popped the two parachutes concealed in the tail of his machine, finally coming to a stop almost four miles from the finish line.

Breedlove climbed out of his machine and waited for his crew to join him. He was anxious to make the return trip—and even more anxious to know what his official time was. The news was not good. His top speed was close to 388 miles per hour. He

Breedlove behind the wheel of his Spirit of America, scorching the Bonneville Salt Flats for a new world speed record.

would have to do much better to break John Cobb's record of 394 miles per hour.

The Spirit of America was refueled and given a quick check. Then with a shrieking roar, Breedlove headed back for the measured mile. This time he did not spare the machine; he opened the throttle wide. The Spirit of America flashed before the eyes of the official timers like a bolt of lightning. Breedlove roared on and then, after several miles of slowing down, finally stopped.

Breedlove knew he had gone faster than on the first run. Had it been fast enough, he wondered, as he stood and waited for his crew and the timers to reach him. As the group arrived, Craig Breedlove could tell by the smiles on their faces that he had been successful. His speed for the second run was very near to an astonishing 428 miles per hour! When this was averaged with the speed of his outward dash, a final mark of 407.45 miles per hour resulted. Breedlove was the new automobile speed king of the world.

Craig Breedlove's achievement on the salt flats on August 5

when he and his Spirit of America set a new world speed record of 407.45 miles per hour was an exhilarating personal triumph. It was the first time an American driver had held the world land speed crown since 1928, when Ray Keech had scorched the sands of Daytona Beach with the White Triplex.

But recognition of Breedlove's achievement by the Fédération Internationale de l'Automobile was quite another matter. This organization, established in the 1940s, had taken over the supervision of all world auto speed record activities. Officials of the federation refused to accept Breedlove's record run for two reasons—his Spirit of America was not an automobile and it was propelled by a non-piston engine.

According to the federation's rules, a vehicle only qualified as an automobile if it had four wheels, two of which were connected to and driven by the car's engine. Further, the engine had to be of the piston type. Of course, at the time these rules were formulated there was no such thing as a turbojet engine, which has no pistons. Breedlove's Spirit of America could meet none of the federation's basic requirements. His vehicle had only three wheels, its turbojet engine was without pistons, and the rear wheels were not driven directly by the engine.

Craig Breedlove did not question the position of the federation. The rules of that governing body were clear enough. He was ready to accept the general feeling that his Spirit of America was actually a motorcycle rather than an automobile. Consequently, it would be more appropriate for his record speed run to come under the rules of the Fédération Internationale Motorcycliste. This world organization, also based in France, establishes the rules for speed contests involving motorcycles. Eventually, it was this international body that gave world recognition to the record set by the young American speedster.

The problems that arose from Breedlove's speed record run did not end with the mark's acceptance by the Fédération Internationale Motorcycliste. The United States Automobile Club also became involved in the matter. After lengthy discussion, officials of the club concluded that while Breedlove's record-breaking vehicle was not an automobile in the strictest sense, nevertheless in view of the revolutionary technical developments that were taking place almost daily, especially with respect to racing cars, a different division ought to be established for the radically designed big boomers. Suiting action to words, the United States Automobile Club created a jet-powered class for automobile speed records. Craig Breedlove's world mark of 407.45 miles per hour was the first to be placed in this new category.

The move by the American auto club was certainly appropriate and timely. Not long after Breedlove pioneered the jet-car speed era, other young, daring drivers followed with equally revolutionary, super-fast machines to challenge the world's speed king.

Craig Breedlove held the world automobile speed crown for a little more than a year. Then the first challengers appeared on the salt flats to bump the speed king from his throne, when the team of Walt Arfons and Tom Green brought their super-powered jet car to Bonneville in the summer of 1964. Called the Wingfoot Express, the racer was typical of the radically advanced vehicles being created for record speed runs. The ultramodern car had a 24-foot-long cylindrical body and a sharply pointed nose. A vertical fin towered above its tail end. Painted blue and silver, the Wingfoot Express was propelled by an enormously powerful turbojet engine. Unlike Breedlove's super-car, the Wingfoot Express rolled on the usual four wheels instead of three.

Tom Green and Walt Arfons spent a good part of the summer of 1964 test-running their big boomer across the salt flats. Try as they would, however, the racer refused to go much over 300 miles per hour. This was far from Breedlove's record and discouraging indeed. Green and Arfons finally decided that the fault lay with the turbojet engine, which was not operating at peak performance.

The Wingfoot Express was rolled back to the shed and a new J-46 turbojet engine, similar to the original, was installed. Again Tom Green took the car out on the salt surface for another series of trial runs. The big boomer's jet exhaust reverberated and thundered over the vast, empty flats. Results were still not too exciting but Arfons and Green decided they would go for a new speed mark on October 2.

Shooting across the measured mile on his first run, Tom Green did a respectable 406 miles per hour. Still, he knew he would have to do a lot better on the return run if he were to break the world speed mark. With his mighty jet engine screeching and rumbling, Green flashed back over the course at an excellent 420 miles per hour. He sent Breedlove's record tumbling into the discard with an average speed of 413.20 miles per hour.

This new record, however, was even more short-lived than Breedlove's. On October 5, three days after Tom Green's record run, Walt's brother Art Arfons took his turn on the salt flats in his Green Monster.

Walt Arfons, brother of Art Arfons, designed and built the Wingfoot Express. Driven by Tom Green, the enormously powerful automobile flashed to a new world land speed record of 413.20 miles per hour in October, 1964.

Long before involving himself in world speed record competition, Art Arfons was a star performer on drag strips. But his talents went much further than merely driving racing cars. He was a wizard at mechanics. If ever a car owed its existence to the efforts of a single individual, the Green Monster did. Art conceived and put together the entire racer, including the turbojet engine. He was forced to. His finances were limited.

Art bought the turbojet engine secondhand; it was a J-79 from an Air Force fighter plane. Discarded, the engine was no longer in operating condition. But having picked it up at a bargain, Art was not discouraged. He hauled it to his backyard garage, bought some technical manuals on the engine, and promptly started to rebuild it. He took the complex power unit apart piece by piece. Every part was cleaned, repaired, or replaced. Then Art put the engine together again in perfect working order.

Engineers who had spent years designing and building turbojets were astonished when they heard what Art Arfons had done. For someone who had never worked on a turbojet engine before, he had performed an extraordinary feat.

This rebuilt turbojet engine was the Green Monster's most outstanding feature. It was an enormously powerful, massive unit. The engine was so big at its tail end that a man could almost stand upright in its opening. Because of the vast amount of air needed by the engine for efficient operation, the front end of the car had as large an opening as the tail pipe. Also among the Green Monster's unusual features was the driver's compartment. This was not in the central part of the vehicle as on most racing cars. Mainly because the giant engine took up so much space, the driver's cockpit, cramped but streamlined, was placed almost on the side of the car. It looked as though the vehicle's designer had forgotten about the driver's compartment in the original plans and at the end had simply stuck it on the side of the body.

To keep his construction costs as low as possible, Art Arfons

The odd-looking, super-fast Green Monster was almost all jet engine on wheels. Arfons drove it from a cramped cockpit on the right side of the body. The airplanelike wing over the front end helped to keep the car on the ground at top speed.

scrounged parts wherever he could find them. He used standard truck axles and suspension systems for attaching the wheels. To prevent the nose of his super-swift racer from soaring into the air while moving at top speed, Art fixed a horizontal wing above it. This was a new development at the time, used by drivers of racing cars on tracks and in cross-country contests. A strong flow of air moving over the wing as the car traveled at high speed developed downward pressing forces, helping to hold the front part of the vehicle on the ground.

If prizes had been awarded for beauty among the big boomers,

Art Arfons's car would never have qualified. Its name was well suited to its appearance, though in fact the Green Monster was painted red, white, and blue. Arfons's only concerns in designing and building the racer had been its power and speed. And results on the salt flats proved that the speedster had known what he was doing.

At Bonneville Salt Flats on October 5, 1964, Arfons first shot over the measured mile at a top speed of slightly over 393 miles per hour; then, on the return run, he clocked an astonishing 475 miles per hour! Averaging the two speeds put the new world speed record at 434.02 miles per hour. Exhausted but happy at the end of the day's hazardous activities, Art told his admiring crew that the Monster had hardly been extended. He had used less than three-quarters of its potential power. Art Arfons was confident that he could ward off any would-be challenger.

A challenger was not long in coming—Craig Breedlove with a reworked and newly streamlined Spirit of America. The most important of the racer's changes was a new and more powerful turbojet engine.

Returning to the salt flats in the late summer of 1964, Breedlove had not needed many trial runs to feel certain that his dream car was ready to regain the speed crown. On October 13, just a week after Art Arfons became the new speed king, Breedlove jumped back into the fray. He boomed over the measured mile course, out and back, for an average speed and new record of 468.72 miles per hour!

To convince challengers that he intended to remain the world's automobile speed king, Breedlove took his Spirit of America out on the course again two days later. Just as John Cobb had felt years previously about his Railton, Breedlove now believed he had hardly scratched the speed potential of his three-wheeled, man-made bolt of lightning. Still keyed up from his achievement of October 13, the daring young driver took his fantastic machine through the course again, determined to find out what its limits really were.

On his first run out over the measured mile stretch, with the turbojet screaming at an earsplitting pitch, Breedlove boomed the Spirit of America over the 500 miles per hour mark! This was a historic moment for super-fast automobiles. On the return run Breedlove opened the throttle to its widest position. It was now or never if he was to know the topmost speed of his dream car.

The one-time dragster flew over the salt course at the unbelievable speed of almost 540 miles per hour! This was the speed range of many jet aircraft. For a wheeled vehicle hugging the earth, it was an incredible velocity. When the two timed speeds were averaged, Craig Breedlove had smashed his own record with a new mark of 526.28 miles per hour.

As he boomed across the end of the mile course on his last run, Breedlove popped the drag 'chutes to begin slowing his racer. But he didn't feel the expected tug. The Spirit of America kept on its course, screaming at near top speed. Breedlove discovered to his horror that the parachutes had torn loose.

Instinctively he slammed his foot on the pedal that operated the mechanical brakes on the rear wheels. Breedlove knew this was a useless move since at the speed of almost 540 miles per hour, the brakes would burn up from friction heat. But he was grasping desperately at anything to help bring his screeching big boomer to a halt.

Shocked, Breedlove realized he was riding an absolutely un-controllable mechanical monster. He tried to keep it on a straight course but the streaking racer veered sharply into an area of soft salt, tearing the wheel from Breedlove's hands.

Swerving in a big arc at a speed of almost 300 miles per hour, the Spirit of America headed for a string of telephone poles. As the first of the poles loomed up rapidly, Breedlove thought, "Well, this is it." He ducked his head as low as possible in the cockpit and waited for the impact. The racer smashed into the wooden pole, snapping it off at ground level as though it were a matchstick. A shower of splinters flew in all directions.

The big boomer continued on its wild course and flew up an embankment. Breedlove and his racer soared some twenty feet into the air like a thrown Frisbee. The machine and driver traveled on their aerial journey for almost two hundred feet and then pitched nose-first into a huge, deep saltwater pool.

By a miracle, Craig Breedlove was still alive and conscious, though badly shaken. He knew he had to get out of the automobile quickly or drown. Breedlove had already pulled the canopy open while sailing through the air. Now he tugged at the safety harness holding him in the driver's seat. Undoubtedly it was this restraint system that had saved his life.

Breedlove scrambled out of his racer and dove into the water. Within a few minutes he had swum to shore and safety. The wild and almost fatal ride was over. Breedlove and his nearly submerged Spirit of America had ended their journey more than three miles from the last marker of the measured mile course.

When his would-be rescuers arrived on the scene, they were amazed to see Breedlove standing on the embankment calmly surveying the remains of his dream car. With hands on hips and smiling, the young driver responded jokingly to anxious queries, "For my next trick I will set myself on fire." *

Art Arfons did not let Breedlove's accident discourage him from trying to beat the sensational new mark. A little less than two weeks after Breedlove's unfortunate mishap, on October 27, Art Arfons took his ungainly Green Monster to the measured mile

* From *The Fastest Men in the World—On Wheels* by Deke Houlgate and Editors of *Auto Racing Magazine* (New York: World Publishing Company/Times Mirror, 1971), page 112.

course. He knew he had only tapped a small measure of his car's enormous power on earlier runs.

And so, after receiving the starter's signal to go, Art Arfons boomed back and forth across the mile course, his turbojet screaming and thundering. When the required two runs were completed, Arfons had the coveted world speed title once more tucked safely in his pocket. He had beaten Craig Breedlove's record by ten miles an hour, for a new mark of 536.71 miles per hour.

Art Arfons's speed record run was the last to be made on the salt flats in the 1964 season. It had been a historic year, one that had witnessed the first automobile traveling in the 500-mile speed range and had then seen the world land speed record broken and

Super-hot gases roar from the tail end of the jet-powered Green Monster as it streaks over the Bonneville Salt Flats. The three dark parallel lines, made with oil, help guide the driver along the speed course.

raised six times. The season had also included a spectacular duel between two daring young drivers, Craig Breedlove and Art Arfons. And the duel was to carry over into the following year.

Almost lost in the fierce competition of the big boomers was the world record of 403.10 miles per hour set by Donald Campbell. Carrying on the racing tradition of his famous father, Donald cracked the world speed mark at Lake Eyre, Australia, on July 17, 1964. His racing machine, also called the Bluebird, was one of the last of the wheel-driven vehicles used to establish a world speed mark.

The repercussions of the sensational speed events on the Bonneville Salt Flats in 1964 carried all the way to Europe and the inner sanctum of the Fédération Internationale de l'Automobile. It was no longer possible for this organization to ignore the incredible machines that were being built and driven by those wild, young American speed demons.

After a period of deliberation, officials of the federation decided to follow in the footsteps of the United States Automobile Club and create a special division for turbojet-powered land vehicles. The speed records made by these unusual machines—including those vehicles called surface effect or hovercraft, as well as jet- and rocket-powered cars—were henceforth to be classed as International Records for Special Vehicles. The very first of these records which the federation recognized was the mark established by Art Arfons at 536 miles per hour.

Although officials of the Fédération Internationale de l'Automobile were willing to change the rules concerning the revolutionary power units of ultramodern racing cars, they were not at all ready to bend with respect to the number of wheels such vehicles should have. They were firm in their stand that an automobile had to have four wheels. Machines with fewer than four wheels had to be classed as motorcycles. It was Craig Breedlove's three-wheeled Spirit of America that brought this matter to the fore.

Following his brush with death, Craig Breedlove had no means of continuing his speed contest with Art Arfons. But Breedlove was determined to regain his speed crown. Returning to his home in California, he immediately laid plans to build a new and more powerful Spirit of America. If all went well, Breedlove hoped to be back on the flats in the fall of 1965.

By the summer of 1965 Breedlove's new racer was completed. Looking every bit as impressive as his first car, the machine was made ready for the trip to Bonneville Salt Flats. The racer had been given a new name to go along with its expected improved performance: Spirit of America-Sonic I. The last portion of the name was significant. It represented Breedlove's hope that the new thunderbolt would be the first automobile to crash through the sound barrier. Aircraft had already done that in the decade following World War II. To surpass sonic speed, the rate at which sound travels under certain conditions of temperature and altitude, Breedlove's new big boomer would have to go at the phenomenal speed of about 740 miles per hour.

Breedlove's new Spirit of America was different from his first racer but equally beautiful in its streamlined appearance. Most important of its different features were the four wheels on which it rolled, rather than three. Breedlove did not intend to have his achievement spoiled by controversy.

Many new ideas arising out of Breedlove's greater experience went into the construction of his second Spirit of America. The racer was much larger and heavier, and the turbojet engine to propel the car was a good deal bigger and more powerful than the one used in the first racer. It was a J-79 turbojet, similar to the type used by Art Arfons in his Green Monster.

Breedlove and his fellow workers used the latest engineering wrinkle from the aeronautical world to enhance the speed of the Spirit of America-Sonic I. The sides of the vehicle's body were made concave, in a shape resembling a Coca-Cola bottle. This

The Spirit of America-Sonic I was designed with concave sides, like the shape of a Coke bottle, for greater speed. The large front opening above the driver's compartment admitted air to the powerful jet engine.

design feature had been developed after thorough wind tunnel tests to make jet aircraft slide through the air faster. The body of the new Spirit of America was fashioned of lightweight but tough Fiberglas and aluminum.

The driver's compartment was at the front of the car, directly below the nose opening for the turbojet engine. The front of the racer ended in a sharp point. A tall vertical fin for stabilizing purposes rose above the tail end. Also at the tail was a large circular opening through which the engine's super-hot gases made their exit.

Craig Breedlove took his new Spirit of America to Bonneville Salt Flats late in the summer of 1965. He lost little time in running the racer through its trial spins. He found out quickly that his new super-car had more than enough speed to retrieve the crown from Art Arfons. But Breedlove also discovered that his powerful big boomer had problems. These would have to be solved before any challenge run could be made.

The body of the new Spirit of America was not as sturdy as its builders had thought, especially when the machine moved at top speed. In certain areas the aluminum and Fiberglas shielding shook and vibrated violently. These trouble spots had to be reinforced, or the hurricane force of the wind pressing against the body at maximum speed would tear it to pieces.

Another problem needing attention was the drag 'chute system. It failed again when Breedlove, scorching the salt desert at a speed of almost 600 miles per hour, tried to slow his racer. Although he nearly met with disaster for a second time because of this braking failure, the young driver managed to control the Spirit of America-Sonic I and bring it to a stop.

It was the end of October before Breedlove and his crew had the racer running to their satisfaction. There wasn't much time left to make the speed effort on the salt flats before winter arrived. Finally, on November 2, the official timers were notified that Craig Breedlove was ready. The former drag strip star's performance did not take long. In a matter of a few minutes, Breedlove had skimmed over the salt flats, first in one direction, then in the opposite, for a sizzling 555.483 miles per hour. This was better than Art Arfons's old mark by a goodly margin; once again Breedlove was the proud holder of the world land speed record.

Arfons was on the scene with his powerful Green Monster that November, waiting to reply to any challenge made by Breedlove. The duel between the two drivers was reaching fever pitch. Within a week after Breedlove cracked the world speed record for auto-

mobiles, Art Arfons had his Green Monster fine-tuned and ready
to roll. Thundering over the measured mile course on November 7,
Arfons topped Breedlove's mark with ease, at 576.553 miles per
hour.

After congratulating his persistent rival and making some adjustments on the Spirit of America-Sonic I, Breedlove took off
on November 15 after Arfons's record. The weather was unex-
pectedly holding good on the flats and there was time to make
one more big run.

Breedlove took his big boomer to about three miles from the
beginning of the measured mile. He revved the engine to a screaming, earthshaking roar. The rumbling noise reverberated over the
barren desert. The racer began to roll. In seconds Breedlove was

*Breedlove's Spirit of America-Sonic I roaring across the Bonne-
ville Salt Flats.*

close to top speed as the first marker on the measured course came into view. With the throttle wide open, the youthful driver flew over the salt course.

On the first run out Breedlove came close to the 600 miles per hour mark he had hoped to pass. Breedlove felt that his Spirit had some speed in reserve, and he was right. On the return dash the former dragster smashed through the 600-mile barrier! It was a tremendous ride. Breedlove had enormous difficulty controlling his machine, which wanted to lift off the ground like an airplane. But he had his speed crown back once more with a record of 600.601 miles per hour. The achievement not only made Craig Breedlove the fastest automobile driver in the world, but also the first man to take an automobile into the 600-mile speed range.

After Breedlove's triumph, there was no time left in the autumn of 1965 for Art Arfons to retaliate. Winter weather arrived, with high winds and rain, putting to an end all high-speed auto runs for that season. But Art Arfons vowed to come back the following year with his Green Monster. He felt positive that his big brute of a machine had more than enough power to overtake Breedlove's record.

Art Arfons took the Green Monster home to South Akron, Ohio, and over the winter months made some adjustments to the turbojet engine which he hoped would improve its performance. He also strengthened the suspension system so the car would hug the ground better at high speed. But there was really not an awful lot that needed attention on the Green Monster. If there had been time before winter arrived, Arfons would have gone after Breedlove's record without any changes to his racer.

A year passed, however, before Art Arfons got back to the salt flats with the Green Monster. On November 17, 1966, he began his challenge run.

He was thundering along at the hair-raising speed of 610 miles per hour when something snapped in the front end of his car.

In a flash, Arfons lost control. The racer jerked viciously to one side, then cartwheeled end over end across the flats. Onlookers were horrified to see pieces of the big boomer tear loose and skim through the air. Arfons was still strapped inside the wildly careening machine as it screeched into a long, slithering slide. The Green Monster, or what was left of it, gouged a deep groove in the salt surface for over a mile before it finally stopped, a broken, battered, twisted hulk of metal.

When rescuers reached the wreck, they were astonished to see Arfons squirming inside it. By incredible good fortune he had survived the wild ride. Ax-wielding crew members chopped furiously to free him. Except for a scratched and bloody face and a severe shaking up, Art was none the worse for his fantastic experience. Parts of the Green Monster were found scattered over miles of the barren flats. A tire was picked up more than three miles from the measured mile course.

The accident put an end to Arfons's world auto speed record attempts. But it did not stop the speedster from dreaming of booming down the mile course one day with a new and revolutionary racer capable of knifing through the sound barrier at a speed of better than 740 miles per hour.

With Art Arfons out of the speed competition, Craig Breedlove seemed content with the world land speed mark he had established. His record remained on the books for five years, until a new and equally youthful racing car driver, Gary Gabelich, came along to try to improve on it.

Gabelich, like Breedlove, was from California and was enormously fascinated with speed. While still in his teens Gabelich had become a first-rate hot rod and drag strip racing car driver, and had then gone on to motorcycle and speedboat racing. At nineteen Gary Gabelich had already held the wheel of a booming turbojet car, guiding it over the salt flats at 350 miles per hour. This taste of riding super-swift racers fired his ambition to drive the fastest automobile in the world. That opportunity came when he was chosen to handle the driver's wheel of the Blue Flame on its record speed attempt.

In its way, the Blue Flame was as revolutionary in construction and operation as the turbojet cars of Breedlove and Arfons had been. Technologically, the Blue Flame was a step in advance of the turbojet-powered big boomers. What made it so was its rocket engine. This power unit was basically similar to those used to send spacecraft into orbit around the earth and astronauts to the moon. Indeed, much of the technical knowledge and skill accumulated during this country's gigantic space program was applied to the design and construction of the Blue Flame.

This swift, space-age, land-based racer owed its existence to

The Blue Flame looked more like a spaceship than an automobile. The driver sat in a small compartment below the tall vertical fin.

The slender, pointed body of the Blue Flame was 38 feet long and stood 8 feet, 8 inches high at the tail. Without fuel the vehicle weighed more than three tons.

many minds and hands. Engineers of Reaction Dynamics were primarily responsible for the design of the racer's compact, powerful rocket engine. The Institute of Gas Technology agreed to provide much of the financial support for building the big boomer. One of the Institute's products, liquefied natural gas, was to be used as fuel for the rocket engine. The Goodyear Tire and Rubber Company designed and made the special tires for the racer. Finally, a group of advanced engineering students of the Illinois Institute of Technology helped create the racing car's slim, streamlined body. Others were also involved before the Blue Flame was pronounced finished and ready for its test runs on the Bonneville Salt Flats.

Every line of the Blue Flame's appearance gave evidence that the racer was truly a product of the space age. If its long, narrow body had been stood on end, it would have looked little different from many of the rocket-powered spacecraft sent aloft from launching pads. Only the wheels attached to the car's body showed that it was intended for use on land and not in space.

The slender, cylindrical aluminum body of the Blue Flame stretched a little more than 38 feet from its sharply pointed nose to its tail. The usual vertical fin, so familiar on big boomers, rose above the tail end. Directly in front of the fin and streamlined into it was the covered compartment for the driver. Two rear wheels were attached to a slender axle about seven feet wide. Two front wheels, less than a foot apart, were partly hidden by the body covering. The front wheels had only a very slight turning radius, just enough for the driver to correct the car if it wandered to the right or left.

The heart of the Blue Flame, its rocket engine, was installed in the tail end of the racer. Though not large, as these units often are, the engine was enormously powerful. Like all reaction power units, its output was measured in pounds of thrust—for this engine the thrust was more than 12,500 pounds. For a conventional engine this would translate into more than 34,000 horsepower. To produce this tremendous power, the unit burned liquefied natural gas and hydrogen peroxide. When these chemicals combined and ignited they generated an incredible propulsion force.

A great deal of thought was given to an effective braking system for this wheeled bullet. In addition to mechanical brakes on the rear wheels, a double series of drag parachutes was installed. Two drag 'chutes were considered sufficient to help the mechanical brakes stop the Blue Flame. In case these failed, however, an extra pair was provided. The Blue Flame's parachutes were carried in a compartment at the tail of the body and could be popped free by the driver.

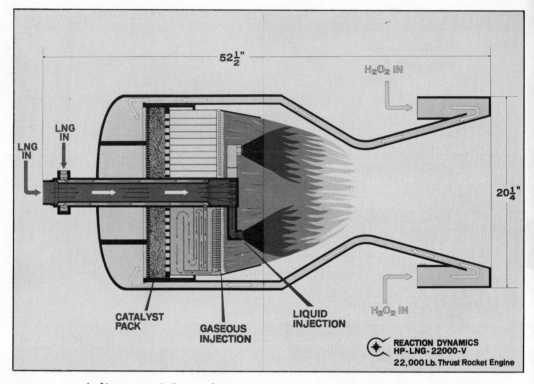

LNG IN

LNG IN

LNG IN

H_2O_2 IN

$52\frac{1}{2}$"

$20\frac{1}{4}$"

CATALYST PACK

GASEOUS INJECTION

LIQUID INJECTION

H_2O_2 IN

REACTION DYNAMICS
HP-LNG-22000-V
22,000 Lb. Thrust Rocket Engine

A diagram of the rocket engine that propelled the Blue Flame to a new world speed record. The engine burned liquefied natural gas, a super-cold form of the gas used for cooking and heating homes. INSTITUTE OF GAS TECHNOLOGY PHOTO

By mid-September of 1970 the Blue Flame, Gary Gabelich, and a small army of engineers and service crew were at Bonneville Salt Flats. The plan was to test the car at ever higher speeds and to judge its performance. If the Blue Flame proved out at the end of the trial runs, it would be sent in quest of the world land speed record.

Not long after the test drives started, mechanical problems cropped up. They were annoyingly time-consuming but not serious. Gary Gabelich carefully took the bullet-swift racer into the

Gary Gabelich, driver of the Blue Flame. Crew members are preparing the vehicle for a test run.

400—the 500—and then in late October into the exhilarating 600 miles per hour range. There was now no question in anybody's mind—both driver and machine were ready for the big run.

Following a few minor, final adjustments to the missile-shaped Blue Flame, it was decided to try for a new speed record on October 23. The day was perfect, with bright sunshine and little wind. The mile course was scraped extra smooth. Timing officials took up their positions. Tension among the engineers and mechanics mounted as Gabelich climbed into his tiny compartment. Crewmen buckled his safety harness, then clamped the overhead canopy tight shut. The great ride was about to begin.

Rocket engines use an enormous amount of fuel in a very short period. Therefore, in order to conserve fuel, a truck was used to push Gabelich to a rolling start. He was not too far from the start of the measured mile; the rocket engine would bring the car to top speed in seconds.

Rolling smoothly and with the starter truck safely out of the way, Gary Gabelich turned on the ignition switch. Instantly huge, billowing clouds of white smoke streaked with orange flame flashed out of the racer's tail. A thunderous roar struck the eardrums of those who were anxiously watching. For a few seconds it seemed that the Blue Flame was hardly moving. Then suddenly, like a shot from a cannon, the racer darted forward at an unbelievable speed. Gabelich flashed over the measured mile in a little less than six seconds—a speed of 617.602 miles per hour! If this could be equalled or bettered on the return dash, Gary Gabelich and the Blue Flame would have established a new world speed record.

Trailing billowing clouds of smoke, Gary Gabelich and the Blue Flame are headed down the Bonneville speed course for a new world land speed record.

Since the rules of the Fédération Internationale de l'Automobile required that in world speed attempts the return run must be made within one hour after the first dash, the crew of the Blue Flame worked swiftly to refuel the racer. The chemical fuels make this a difficult procedure to do in a hurry. But Gabelich's men did their job well and had some minutes to spare. The young driver quickly got his powerful machine moving and, again trailing billowing clouds of smoke and fire, zoomed over the measured mile.

The spectators thought the return run had been even faster than the first. Their feelings were confirmed by the official timers who announced that Gary Gabelich had streaked over the course for his two runs at a new world land speed mark of 622.407 miles per hour!

This was a phenomenal velocity for a landbound vehicle and everyone connected with designing and building the Blue Flame was supremely happy. No further effort was made that season by Gary Gabelich with the Blue Flame to improve on the record or to break through the sound barrier. The young star of the drag strip circuits was satisfied with having pushed the world auto land speed record to an astonishing new high.

Chapter 8
Tomorrow's Quest

Gary Gabelich's 622 miles per hour represents the high-water mark in the ceaseless quest for automotive speed. The land speed record is now at the edge of the sound barrier, long since crossed by airmen. Will drivers of swift, land-based cars also be able to pass it? No one in the automobile world can give a definite answer to this question. Indeed, no one can say with any certainty what would happen to a driver or a car that rocketed through the sound barrier.

Guesses have been made that the driver would not be able to withstand the enormous physical strains that his body would be subjected to. Also, it has been said that the racer would fly apart at speeds of more than 740 miles per hour. The only sure prediction, it seems, is that at some future time a fearless young driver is going to attempt to find out. Why? Again there are no sure answers.

Many in the automotive field find it difficult to see what, if anything, of practical usefulness could come out of the creation of a supersonic automobile. They see little purpose in expending the vast technical effort and huge sum of money such a car would require.

Others, with an opposite viewpoint, feel that building such a vehicle could lead to auto improvements for the use of the general public: better tires, a better braking system, even a revolutionary non-polluting automobile engine. Still others feel that the supersonic automobile will be built and test-driven simply because of the way human beings think and feel. A compulsion to undertake hazardous ventures plus a never-ending curiosity about the unknown will almost certainly make people keep trying to drive an automobile faster than the speed of sound.

A number of years have passed since Gary Gabelich established a new world speed mark for automobiles. It is still on the record books at this writing. No one has tried to displace him as the speed king. But there are lots of plans and construction involving ultramodern racers that may be faster than the Blue Flame. Little is known about these activities because the individuals concerned prefer to work in secrecy. But there are rumors of what is going on. One concerns an automobile capable of streaking over the ground at twice the speed of sound—an incredible 1400 miles per hour!

Should any of these super-swift big boomers see the light of day, they will not be American machines exclusively. Persistent rumors say that similarly fast vehicles are in the works in Russia, Australia, and Japan. Only the future will tell whether any of these lightning-swift motor cars will come into existence and lead to the crowning of a new world land speed king.

Chronology of World Land Speed Records

SPEED M.P.H.	DATE	DRIVER	CAR	PLACE
39.24	12/18/1898	Chasseloup-Laubat	Jeantaud	Achères, France
41.42	1/17/1899	Jenatzy	Jenatzy	Achères, France
43.69	1/17/1899	Chasseloup-Laubat	Jeantaud	Achères, France
49.92	1/27/1899	Jenatzy	Jenatzy	Achères, France
57.60	3/4/1899	Chasseloup-Laubat	Jeantaud	Achères, France
65.79	4/29/1899	Jenatzy	Jenatzy	Achères, France
75.06	4/13/1902	Serpollet	Serpollet	Nice, France
76.08	8/5/1902	Vanderbilt	Mors	Ablis, France
76.60	11/5/1902	Fournier	Mors	Dourdan, France
77.13	11/17/1902	Augiéres	Mors	Dourdan, France
83.47	7/17/1903	Duray	Gobron-Brillié	Ostend, Belgium
84.73	11/5/1903	Duray	Gobron-Brillié	Dourdan, France
91.37	1/12/1904	Ford	Ford Arrow	Lake St. Clair, Michigan
92.30	1/27/1904	Vanderbilt	Mercedes	Daytona Beach, Florida

SPEED M.P.H.	DATE	DRIVER	CAR	PLACE
94.78	3/31/1904	Rigolly	Gobron-Brillié	Nice, France
97.26	5/25/1904	de Caters	Mercedes	Ostend, Belgium
103.55	7/21/1904	Rigolly	Gobron-Brillié	Ostend, Belgium
104.52	11/13/1904	Baras	Darracq	Ostend, Belgium
104.65	1/25/1905	Macdonald	Napier	Daytona Beach, Florida
109.65	12/30/1905	Héméry	Darracq	Arles-Salon, France
127.66	1/23/1906	Marriott	Stanley Rocket	Daytona Beach, Florida
131.72	3/23/1910	Oldfield	Blitzen Benz	Daytona Beach, Florida
141.37	4/23/1911	Burman	Blitzen Benz	Daytona Beach, Florida
149.86	2/17/1919	de Palma	Packard	Daytona Beach, Florida
146.16*	9/25/1924	Campbell	Sunbeam	Pendine Sands, Wales
150.87	7/21/1925	Campbell	Sunbeam	Pendine Sands, Wales
152.33	3/16/1926	Segrave	Sunbeam	Southport Sands, England
169.30	4/28/1926	Thomas	Babs Higham	Pendine Sands, Wales
171.02	4/29/1926	Thomas	Babs Higham	Pendine Sands, Wales
174.88	2/4/1927	Campbell	Bluebird Napier	Pendine Sands, Wales
203.79	3/29/1927	Segrave	Sunbeam	Daytona Beach, Florida
206.96	2/19/1928	Campbell	Bluebird Napier	Daytona Beach, Florida
207.55	4/22/1928	Keech	White Triplex	Daytona Beach, Florida

* By 1925 an average of two runs was required for world speed records. De Palma's higher speed in 1919 was a single run.

SPEED M.P.H.	DATE	DRIVER	CAR	PLACE
231.44	3/11/1929	Segrave	Golden Arrow	Daytona Beach, Florida
246.09	2/5/1931	Campbell	Bluebird Napier	Daytona Beach, Florida
253.97	2/24/1932	Campbell	Bluebird Napier	Daytona Beach, Florida
272.46	2/23/1933	Campbell	Bluebird Rolls-Royce	Daytona Beach, Florida
276.82	3/7/1935	Campbell	Bluebird Rolls-Royce	Daytona Beach, Florida
301.13	9/3/1935	Campbell	Bluebird Rolls-Royce	Bonneville Salt Flats, Utah
312.00	11/19/1937	Eyston	Thunderbolt	Bonneville Salt Flats, Utah
345.50	8/27/1938	Eyston	Thunderbolt	Bonneville Salt Flats, Utah
350.20	9/15/1938	Cobb	Railton	Bonneville Salt Flats, Utah
357.50	9/16/1938	Eyston	Thunderbolt	Bonneville Salt Flats, Utah
369.70	8/23/1939	Cobb	Railton	Bonneville Salt Flats, Utah
394.20	9/16/1947	Cobb	Railton-Mobil Special	Bonneville Salt Flats, Utah
407.45	8/5/1963	Breedlove	Spirit of America*	Bonneville Salt Flats, Utah
403.10**	7/17/1964	Campbell	Bluebird	Lake Eyre, Australia
413.20	10/2/1964	Green	Wingfoot Express	Bonneville Salt Flats, Utah
434.02	10/5/1964	Arfons	Green Monster	Bonneville Salt Flats, Utah
468.72	10/13/1964	Breedlove	Spirit of America	Bonneville Salt Flats, Utah

* Three wheels and jet-propelled—first of the special big boomers.
** The last record set by a wheel-driven automobile.

SPEED M.P.H.	DATE	DRIVER	CAR	PLACE
526.28	10/15/1964	Breedlove	Spirit of America	Bonneville Salt Flats, Utah
536.71	10/27/1964	Arfons	Green Monster	Bonneville Salt Flats, Utah
555.483	11/2/1965	Breedlove	Spirit of America —Sonic I	Bonneville Salt Flats, Utah
576.553	11/7/1965	Arfons	Green Monster	Bonneville Salt Flats, Utah
600.601	11/15/1965	Breedlove	Spirit of America —Sonic I	Bonneville Salt Flats, Utah
622.407	10/23/1970	Gabelich	Blue Flame*	Bonneville Salt Flats, Utah

* First of the rocket-powered, record-breaking big boomers.

Further Reading

Ayling, Keith. *Gas, Guts and Glory.* New York: Abelard-Schuman, 1970.

Borgeson, Griffith. *The Golden Age of the American Racing Car.* New York: W. W. Norton & Company, Inc., 1966.

Engle, Lyle Kenyon, and Editors of *Auto Racing Magazine. Road Racing in America.* New York: Dodd, Mead & Company, 1971.

Hough, Richard. *Racing Cars.* London: Paul Hamlyn, Ltd., 1966.

Houlgate, Deke, and Editors of *Auto Racing Magazine. The Fastest Men in the World—On Wheels.* New York: World Publishing Company/ Times Mirror, 1971.

Posthumus, Cyril. *Land Speed Record—A Complete History of World Record-Breaking Cars from 39.24 to 600+ MPH.* New York: Crown Publishers, Inc., 1972.

Index